UNDERSTANDING
CEMETERY SYMBOLS

A FIELD GUIDE FOR

Historic Graveyards

BY TUI SNIDER

T0401693

ABOUT THE COVER PHOTOS

Writing research takes me to historic graveyards all over the world, and I love taking pictures of these beautiful open-air museums.

To see more of my photos, read articles about cemetery symbols, and to grab your *FREE* copy of a "Quick Guide to the Many Meanings of Hands in Historic Cemeteries," visit my website: TuiSnider.com.

ABOUT THE AUTHOR

Tui Snider is an award-winning author, photographer, musician, and speaker who specializes in offbeat travel, cemetery symbols, and haunted lore. As she says: "I used to write fiction. But then, I moved to Texas!"

Snider's writing and photography have been featured by a variety of outlets, including *Coast to Coast AM, FOX Travel News, LifeHack, Sky Europe, easyJet,* the City of Plano and many more.

Snider's award winning books inspired by the Lone Star state include *Paranormal Texas, The Lynching of the Santa Claus Bank Robber*, and *Unexpected Texas.*

In 2016, Tui served as the Writer in Residence for Tarleton State University's *Langdon Review.* She recently taught classes based on her books at Texas Christian University.

Tui has several new

Tui Snider exploring the cemeteries of New Orleans

projects in progress, including companion journals for this book (*Graveyard Journal: A Workbook for Exploring Historic Cemeteries*, and *Ghost Hunters Journal: A Workbook for Paranormal Investigators*) as well as a book about quirky burial sites and the stories behind them . To find out when these books will be released, and to keep up with all of Tui's projects, sign up for her private newsletter over at TuiSnider.com

Tui enjoys connecting with readers all over the world. If you're on Twitter, Instagram, Facebook or Pinterest, follow her and say hi.

ACKNOWLEDGMENTS

I f you'll pardon the pun, writing *Understanding Cemetery Symbols* was a tremendous undertaking! I never would have been able to publish this book without the kindness, encouragement, and assistance I received from the following: Craig Rahanian, Bob Snider, Woofmutt, The StoryDam Twitter chat peeps, Joy Daley, Shelly Tucker, Bambi Harris, Naomi Morlan, Laura Douglas, Raymond Huyghe, Teal Gray, Russ, Patty, Mike, and David "Sumoflam" Kravetz.

I'm also grateful to everyone who chatted with me at the 2017 Southern Monument Builders Conference, especially: Sammie Peters, Kirsten Trudo, Dodi Campbell, and Rusty Brenner.

A huge thank you also goes out to members of my Launch Team, who continue to help me spread the word about my writing: Teal Gray, Alycia Forbes, Donna McNicol, Christa Monaco, Judith Brumm, Sheila Gay, Deb Atwood, Tim Fooks, Kerry Dewbre, Jeri Martin, Nicole Rivera, Denise Young, Anna ES, Amanda Malm, Patricia Lynne, Paula Puffer, Ed Wetterman, Jay Gillis, Brenda Newby, Georgina Holzmeier, Heidi Fountain, Kit Cameron, Julie Reeser , Susan Hill, Sierra Nyokka, Laura Irrgang, Jan Dotter Gomes, Linda Anthony Hill, Melissa Blaine, and Steven Malone.

I'd also like to thank every single person who ever visited my blog, said hi on Facebook, or RT'd me on Twitter!

DEDICATION

To my ever-loving hubby, Larry, my graveyard buddies (Teal Gray, Laura Douglas & Shelly Tucker) & Eddie Hargrave:
If Heaven has books, I know you're reading them all!

CONTENTS

1 WHY SYMBOLS MATTER

P eople often assume our ancestors used symbolism on their tombstones because they were illiterate. You don't have to know how to read, after all, to understand a symbol.

A HIGHLY LITERATE NATION

While researching this book, I looked at US literacy rates throughout history. Although the exact numbers are hard to pin down, I was surprised to see how high the numbers were.

For example, from 1650-1670, the literacy rate in New England is estimated at nearly 60%. By 1795, this number climbed to 90%. Even more impressive, many historians claim that Boston's literary rate was nearly 100% during this time period.

Of course, these literacy figures only take upper class white males of the time period into account. It's hard to say what the literacy rate was for women, and the poor. As for slaves, in many parts of the United States it was illegal for them to learn how to read until much later.

Even so, the hey day for cemetery symbolism in America's historic graveyards spans roughly from 1830 to 1910. Literacy rates at this time are estimated to be anywhere from 90 to 97%.

So, while it is beyond the scope of this book to delve into all the intricacies of literacy in America, suffice it to say that we are, and have always been, a highly literate nation.

WHAT'S SO GREAT ABOUT SYMBOLS ANYWAY?

Often, when I tell people how much I enjoy researching cemetery symbolism, they react as if I've joined the Illuminati or some other mysterious secret society. In reality, there is nothing weird or arcane about using symbols.

All of us use symbols each and every day. For instance, we see a red octagon at the corner of the street while we're driving, so we stop. A friend texts us by phone to ask how our job interview went and we reply with an emoticon, such as :) to symbolize a smile, or :(to indicate a frown. Symbols are a quick and easy substitute for written words. But there can be much more to them than that.

I learned a lot while researching this book. Obviously, I learned a lot about cemetery symbols. More than that, however, I realized that our relationship with symbols has changed dramatically since the first European settlers set foot on this continent.

To explain, let me back up and define symbols again. Simply put, symbols are the perfect example of the old cliche that "a picture is worth a thousand words."

There is, however, a deeper way to connect with and use symbols. This is what makes them so fascinating, and even powerful.

When we are deeply connected to a symbol, it takes a bunch of complex ideas and communicates them instantly. When you look at a symbol that you are deeply connected to, it's like a visual download, and can even elicit strong feelings.

Here's an example every American can relate to: our country's flag. Obviously, the American flag is not a sentient being. However, if you saw someone rip or burn one, I bet that not only would you be upset, but it would affect you physically. I'm sure that your blood pressure would increase, at the very least.

On the other hand, when you attend an event where the national anthem is played while the American flag is lowered or raised, I bet you feel something inside of yourself, as well. Personally, there are times when attending a flag ceremony has brought tears to my eyes!

This is what I mean when I refer to a deep connection to a symbol. What I noticed while researching this book is that from the beginning, right up through the Victorian Era, Americans were deeply acquainted with a wide variety of symbols.

While it's true we still use symbols in modern cemeteries, we tend to use them in very literal ways, rather than in deeper ways, such as we do with our flag.

For example, if I see a rooster engraved on a modern headstone, I can pretty much assume the deceased had a fondness for chickens.

When seen on older monuments, however, I think of how, symbolically, the rooster represents vigilance, awakening and resurrection. Also, the reason roosters often adorn weather vanes is to signify how male chickens keep an eye out for evil both day and night. So a rooster may appear on the headstone for the eldest male in the family, not simply because roosters are male, but because this man was responsible for protecting his family.

Furthermore, if the rooster is shown standing near a

male figure, I can assume that I'm looking at a statue of St. Peter. The rooster, in this case, refers to the time Jesus told St. Peter that, "The cock shall not crow, till thou has denied me thrice."

That's a lot of ideas wrapped up in one little bird, right?

On a similar note, in historic cemeteries, a squirrel holding an acorn symbolizes spiritual striving and meditation. When you see the same statue in a modern burial ground, however, it probably just means that the person thought squirrels were cute.

I could go on and on, but I'll just give you one more. On a modern headstone, a horse's bridle likely means that the deceased enjoyed riding horses. On a historic headstone, however, a bridle and bit symbolize control over one's less than saintly urges.

So getting back to the assumption that our ancestors used symbols because they were illiterate is not the case. In fact, from what I can tell, our ancestors were deeply connected to many more symbols than we are today. If that's the case, then who are the truly illiterate ones?

CONTEXT IS IMPORTANT

Another thing to keep in mind when pondering cemetery symbols is that their meaning depends on the time, place, and belief system of those using it. The rooster, squirrel, and bridle I just mentioned are good examples of symbols meaning different things in different time periods, but you also have to be aware of the belief systems involved.

Pitchers, for instance, mean different things depending on where you are. If you are visiting a Jewish cemetery, then a pitcher at a grave site implies that the person descended from the tribe of Levi. (Levites washed the hands of their priests with water.)

If you are in the Christian section of a historic graveyard, a pitcher most likely represents a woman of strong moral character, someone who was exceedingly generous, self-sacrificing, and charitable. She may even have been involved in America's Temperance movement, so check the dates on the headstone to see if she lived during the Prohibition Era (1920 – 1933.)

SYMBOLIC MEANING IS NOT SET IN STONE

Sometimes, the meaning of a symbol changes drastically over the centuries. It starts out meaning one thing, and then winds up meaning the exact opposite. A good example of this is the swastika. To those of us living in the 21st century, the swastika is a symbol of hatred.

This wasn't always the case. The swastika has been around for millennia, used by different cultures all over the world, even in America. For instance, several Southwest Indian tribes use the swastika as part of their creation myth. I visited a museum in Arizona where Native American baskets featuring swastika designs were on display, along with a carefully worded explanation letting viewers know that their use of this ancient symbol has absolutely nothing to do with Nazism or Adolph Hitler.

So in addition to being aware of a symbol's context in time and place, you need to understand the belief system behind it. Symbols can be a lot of fun to research, but it's best not to assume too much about anyone and the reasons behind why they use a certain symbol. For this reason, I sometimes joke that when it comes to cemetery symbols, "Just because it's written in stone, doesn't always mean that it's written in stone."

2 HOW TO USE THIS BOOK

In this day of high-tech everything, it seems condescending to explain how to use a regular old paperback book, right? I must confess that when I see a "How to use this book" section in a Table of Contents, I often skip over it, or at least, roll my eyes.

So feel free to skip over this section, or at least roll your eyes, as I briefly explain how this particular book is set up. It's fairly self-explanatory, but there are few things that may not make sense at first glance.

First off, I should let you know that while *Understanding Cemetery Symbols* is the result of several years of serious research, I have been interested in old cemeteries for as long as I can remember. In fact, when I was 9-years-old and a creepy janitor tried to kidnap me and my friend, we made our escape by running through an old graveyard.

These days, writing research often takes me to historic cemeteries, and it's so much fun! To me, cemeteries are open-air museums where a person can peacefully enjoy art and nature. I am excited to share this passion with you, and I truly hope this book inspires you to explore the area near you.

HOW THIS BOOK IS ORGANIZED

When I first began organizing my research, I thought the

finished product would simply consist of a brief introduction followed by a lengthy A to Z listing of cemetery symbols. The more I worked on that style of book, however, the less I liked it.

As you can tell by the Table of Contents, I wound up dividing my research into several categories. For instance, there are separate chapters for plants, humans figures, crosses, types of monuments, architectural styles, and so on. Only at the end do I have chapter called "Miscellaneous Cemetery Symbols from A to Z."

As I've learned by using my own favorite reference books, the more you use them, the more helpful they become. So before you take this book out to a historic graveyard, take a few minutes to acquaint yourself with the way the information is arranged.

WHAT'S LEFT OUT OF THIS BOOK

The history of cemetery symbolism is a huge topic. People have been dying for a very long time, after all, and it doesn't look like they will quit any time soon. While I've learned a lot about the subject, my own research is ongoing.

Even after narrowing the focus of this guide down to the United States, I realize that this book does not explain every single cemetery symbol you will ever see.

There are thousands of Catholic saints, for instance. So when I wrote Chapter 13 "Saints, Angels, and Other Beings," I did my best to include the ones you are most likely to find in American cemeteries.

The same goes for Chapter 14 So Many Crosses! The chapter title says it all, really. Not only are there well over 300 different types of crosses, but nearly every cross goes by at least four different names.

And don't even get me started on Chapter 16 "Clubs, Secret Societies & Organizations." Considering that at one time there were over 2000 active fraternal organizations in America, you can see how I needed to pick and choose the ones to include in this guide.

In other words, cemetery symbolism is a great big subject. Every single chapter could easily be expanded into an entire book of its own.

COMPANION WORKBOOKS

In spite of a rather pointed epitaph I saw in Key West claiming that, "If you're reading this, you desperately need a hobby," I think exploring cemeteries is a wonderful pastime. For starters, it gets you out into nature and it helps you connect with history.

So in addition to this book, I have created two companion workbooks: *Graveyard Journal: A Workbook for Exploring Historic Cemeteries*, and *Ghost Hunters Journal: A Workbook for Paranormal Investigators*.

The *Graveyard Journal* is a workbook for keeping track of all the cemeteries you visit. It has room to record the details for up to 50 different burial grounds.

The *Ghost Hunters Journal*, on the other hand, is a place for paranormal investigators to keep track of the various experiences they have, whether they are in a haunted cemetery or elsewhere.

Even if you don't use my companion workbooks, it's a good idea to write down the details of your cemetery visits. Details can get fuzzy over time. You may forget which cemetery has your favorite angel statue, where the key to the graveyard gate is kept, or which farm to market road leads to your favorite country burial ground.

And finally, the most important tip I can suggest for using this book is to keep it in the glovebox of your car or tucked in your purse so it will be handy when you are driving by a historic cemetery and you have a little time to kill.

I've really done my best to make this book a useful tool. I hope you enjoy it! Also, if you end up posting any photos online from your cemetery visits, please tag them with #TuiSnider #GraveHour and/or @TuiSnider, so that I can enjoy them and respond to you.

OK, let's get started!

3 AMERICAN BURIAL LANDSCAPE

J ust as houses and cities shape our terrain, human burial grounds shape our landscape. Let enough time pass, and a prehistoric burial mound simply becomes a hill to local inhabitants. Even today, it is quite possible to drive through a seemingly natural landscape and not realize that many of its geographic features were actually manmade!

PREHISTORIC BURIAL MOUNDS

Well before any European settlers arrived on the shores of America, its landscape was shaped by the Native Americans living here, ancient tribes dating back as early as 250-150 BC. A big part of their geographic impact was due to their burial customs.

Well over 500 different Native American tribes once dwelled throughout the United States, and their burial rituals and beliefs were varied. Even so, the way humans deal with their dead depends a lot on whether they are nomadic or village dwelling.

Nomadic tribes, such as those living in the American Plains and the Pacific Northwest, usually left their dead to be reclaimed by nature in one form or another. Bodies were placed on raised scaffolds, tucked inside cedar trees, or otherwise offered to the elements so they could be reclaimed by nature. This kind of arrangement does not require a marker nor does it create a cemetery or centralized place to visit the dead.

On the other hand, village-dwelling Native Americans developed different burial customs, including manmade hill-like structures called burial mounds. As the name implies, a burial mound is created by heaping dirt onto a grave or group of graves. Native American burial mounds range in height from a mere 3-feet to a looming 90-feet-tall. The most common style is conical, rather like a dirt pyramid, but they sometimes had ambitious designs, and could be shaped like animals or arranged in fancy geometric patterns.

It's also interesting to note that just as in ancient Egypt, it appears to archeologists that upon the death of an important leader, animals, servants and maybe even family members were sacrificed and buried inside the burial mound along with him. Also jewelry, pottery, and other goods were often placed inside these mounds to honor the leader.

Even well into the 1800's, Americans were quite aware of the impact ancient Native American burial mounds had upon the landscape.

NATIVE AMERICAN BURIAL CAIRNS

Cairns are another Native American burial feature that all too easily blends into the landscape and can be overlooked. Rocks in a cluster or pile are called "cairns," a term which comes from an old Scottish word meaning "heap of stones."

Native American burial cairns are often found in the most scenic places, such as the tops of hills and mountains. Archeologists speculate that this was meant to offer the deceased a better view, or to place them closer to sky-dwelling deities, but they do not always know for sure.

Caddo Indian burial mound in Alto, Texas

Even today, hikers may inadvertently stumble upon Native American burial cairns while exploring the land and taking in scenic views.

These days, farming and urban development have changed the landscape so drastically that, unless the area has been set aside as a national park or otherwise labeled, we are mostly unaware of which geographic structures around us were shaped by prehistoric humans.

SPANISH EXPLORERS

Early Spanish explorers were next on the American scene. An explorer's life is typically nomadic, so when members of a team died, they were buried along the way and with little fanfare. Bodies were buried without a coffin, and were often unmarked. If they were marked, it was with a small cairn and/or a small wooden cross.

American's oldest city, St. Augustine, was founded by

Spaniards along the northern coast of Florida in 1565. The city's inhabitants quickly built a Catholic church, and in keeping with European traditions of the time, the deceased were buried inside the church building. Once again, coffins were not used. Bodies were simply wrapped in cloth, a few floor planks pried up, and the remains were laid to rest directly beneath the pews.

Since no markers were placed on the floor, nor records kept, archeologists find it challenging to know exactly who was buried in these churches, or when. It is known that the higher you ranked in society, the closer you would be buried to the altar, so a body's position in the church can be an important clue.

After a while, however, the church floor became too crowded to bury any more parishioners there. At this point, the citizens of St. Augustine began burying people in the graveyard surrounding the church.

EUROPEAN SETTLERS

In 1620, the Mayflower landed at Plymouth Rock, bringing with it the next group of people to influence the burial customs of America. These Pilgrims were no strangers to harsh realities, and over the course of their first winter here they buried 52 out of the initial 102 settlers.

Like the ancient Romans, Pilgrims buried their dead at night. In fact, the word "funeral" comes from *funeralis,* the Latin word for a torch. Torches were needed to light the way to the graveyard during a burial. It's also speculated that the Pilgrims' nighttime burial custom may have given them the added advantage of not allowing Native Americans to realize how badly they were faring.

VICTORIAN ERA MONUMENTS

America's Civil War stretched from 1861 - 1865, and over the course of those four long years, more than 620,000 soldiers, both Confederate and Union, died. To put this in perspective, if you add the total amount of soldiers slain in every other battle the United States has engaged in, the grand total is only slightly higher, at 644,000 total lives lost. So in the years surrounding the Civil War, it was a rare person who did not bury a close family member or loved one due to that conflict. It's fair to say that America was a nation in mourning.

Meanwhile in England, after Queen Victoria's husband died in 1861, the queen went into deep mourning. British subjects followed Queen Victoria's lead and from this, highly structured rituals and rules of etiquette for mourners came about. Death was romanticized in popular literature and artwork of the era. Even those who were about to die were encouraged to practice "the good death" by gracefully accepting their fate. So while it may seem that Americans were a bit obsessed with death during the Victorian Era, you can hardly blame them.

Rather than being a private affair, mourning during the Victorian Era was not only something you wanted others in your community to be aware of, but it was nearly a competitive sport. People took notice of and gossiped accordingly about those who mourned properly, and those who did not.

As the railroad spread across the United States, this allowed high quality granite and marble to be shipped around the country for memorialists to engrave. During this time, those who could afford it erected grand monuments with lengthy poetic epitaphs and meaningful symbols

Scraped graves in Denson Cemetery near Grapeland, TX

engraved upon them.

SCRAPED GRAVES IN THE RURAL SOUTH

Lush green lawns have become such a common feature of today's burial grounds that if you could travel back in time to the 1800's for a graveyard tour through the rural South, you might be in for a shock. It's easy to forget that the first lawn mower wasn't invented until 1830. Even then, lawn grasses weren't developed by the US Department of Agriculture until the 1930's, a good 100 years later.

To early settlers, grass had different connotations than it does today. Not only could it harbor bugs and snakes, but in the days before lawn sprinklers, a large expanse of dried grass could be a fire hazard. Just as a homesteader's cabin often had dirt floors, their yards, as well, were often kept free of vegetation.

By the same token, early cemeteries throughout the South were often scraped clean of plant life. This practice spread throughout 19th century cemeteries in Alabama, Georgia, Louisiana, and Texas.

Historians now think this practice came to America through the influence of African Americans, since a similar custom of scraped burial grounds with mounded graves is seen along the slave coast of Africa. It's assumed that the custom then gained popularity throughout the South due to its practical aspects.

Over time, however, people forgot the original how and why behind this tradition began and simply assumed it was a way of showing respect for the dead.

Although dozens of scraped burial grounds still existed throughout the South as late as the 1990's, few, if any, remain today. You may still, however, find a few graves here and there that are covered in gravel or mounded up and decorated with shells. When you find graves like this, you are likely standing in one of these formerly scraped grave cemeteries that has since been covered with grass.

FAMILY TENDED PLOTS

Scraped earth or not, it was the responsibility of the deceased person's family to maintain their grave. For this reason, family plots were clearly marked so people knew exactly which area they were in charge of maintaining.

Throughout the 19th century annual cemetery cleanup days, often called "Decoration Day" or "Homecoming," were the norm, especially in rural communities. In the 1800's these cleanup days were major social events for the community. These were festive gatherings, with picnics, prayers, and even games and frivolity for children and adults. In this way, the maintenance and upkeep of the community cemetery allowed people to maintain social ties with the living, while also paying respect to the dead.

As families have scattered, annual cemetery cleanup parties are not as common or as big of a community event as they once were. Sometimes you will see information about these events posted by the cemetery gates or outbuildings. Even today, in smaller rural communities, many historic cemeteries rely on volunteers for maintenance.

After the Great Depression, the American populace became more mobile. Many families became scattered geographically and were not always able to return home to maintain family plots. Because of our changing society, the idea of "perpetual care" came was developed. Perpetual care means that when you buy a burial plot, you also pay a fee towards having the cemetery maintain the grounds.

MEANWHILE IN THE CITY

From the time of the Pilgrims right on through the 1700's, American city dwellers were buried in churchyards. As cities grew in population and became more crowded, so did these urban burial grounds. This was especially troublesome during epidemics, when the yards were hastily filled with new bodies.

From time to time a churchyard wall would weaken from flood or other deterioration, and this would send piles of rotting corpses tumbling onto the streets. Not only was this a horrifying sight, but it smelled awful and helped to spread disease.

As American cities grew in population, real estate prices soared. So not only were corpse-filled churchyards an eyesore, but they took up valuable space.

Meanwhile, European city dwellers faced a similar dilemma. To remedy the situation, in 1804 Parisians created a lush, well-landscaped burial ground beyond the city limits. Called Pere La Chaise, this became the world's first garden cemetery, and it remains a popular tourist destination to this day.

BIRTH OF AMERICA'S GARDEN CEMETERY

Inspired by the success of the French, the city of Boston hired a team of architects and designers to create something similar. In 1831, Mount Auburn Cemetery in Cambridge, Massachusetts opened its gates to the public as the first garden cemetery in America. It was such a hit that other cities around the nation soon followed suit.

While the original goal for garden cemeteries was to rid the city of its dead, they became highly popular with the living, as well. These days, a cemetery rarely tops our list for weekend destinations, but during the Victorian Era, a day spent at a garden cemetery was far from morbid. City dwellers packed picnics so they could spend a relaxing day out in nature. Hunters shot game while artists set up easels and painted landscapes. Some garden cemeteries even hosted public festivals and carriage races! In fact, it was the success of these garden cemeteries that inspired America's first public parks.

Over time, people began using these parks for recreation and visiting cemeteries only for mourning and funerals. As infant mortality rates dropped and life spans have increased, American's relationship with death has changed.

People rarely die at home now, for instance, or have wakes or funerals in their parlors as they once did. Barring accidents, nowadays most people die in hospitals or nursing homes. Modern people tend to avoid cemeteries unless they are attending a funeral. Even after our loved ones are buried, many of us rarely return to visit them. Death has become something most of us can ignore until the moment it strikes.

MODERN BURIAL OPTIONS

Throughout the 20th century, Americans were either buried or cremated, with few options in between. As we move into the 21st century, however, environmentally friendly options, called "green burials," are becoming much more varied and accepted. Some of these options eschew the idea of a permanent headstone. Instead, they purposely opt for grave markers that will disintegrate over time.

Also, perhaps inspired by the holograms on Star Trek TV shows and movies, there are even companies developing high tech memorials. These offer graveside access to photos, movies, and other memorabilia chosen by the deceased and their families as a remembrance.

GARDEN CEMETERY RENAISSANCE

Perhaps more importantly, Americans are beginning to realize once again that burial grounds exist to nurture the living as well as shelter the dead. In recent decades, for example, many of America's original garden cemeteries, including Mt. Auburn, have been placed on the historical register.

In addition, historic cemeteries across the country now offer historic tours, annual festivals and events which run

Old City Cemetery, Biloxi, MS

the gamut from jazz picnics, costumed reenactments, performances of Shakespeare, and more.

Others offer birding tours, and since the shrubs and flowers planted during the Victorian Era are now a source for heritage bulbs and plantings, some have applied for arboretum status. In this way, America's garden cemeteries have become living libraries.

In the 1960's, Harvard professor turned hippie, Timothy Leary, famously urged people to "tune in, turn on and drop out." These days, with our fancy phones and other smart devices, we spend so much time tuned in and turned on, that perhaps a better cry for our time might be to "unplug, unwind and take a quiet stroll through a beautiful historic graveyard."

4 CEMETERY SAFETY & ETIQUETTE

After reading this far, I hope you are excited to take this book and visit your nearest historic cemetery! (And if you decide to post photos online of the experience, remember to tag them with @TuiSnider, #TuiSnider and/or #GraveHour, so I can enjoy them and respond to you.)

Before we head to the graveyard, however, there are a few things to keep in mind, such as safety and etiquette. While being a taphophile is nowhere near as dangerous as skydiving or spelunking, exploring historic graveyards comes with its own set of dangers and considerations.

CEMETERY SAFETY

AVOID CRITTERS & CRIMINALS: Every graveyard is different. When traipsing through historic graveyards in sparsely populated areas such as West Texas, I keep my eyes out for fire ants and rattlesnakes. However, when poking around an old churchyard in a major city, other humans are a bigger concern than wildlife. Sadly, urban graveyards can be havens for drug users and even criminals.

TAKE A BUDDY: Personally, I *never* visit graveyards alone, especially after dark. Many urban cemeteries are dangerous at night due to criminal activity of one sort or another. Some are dangerous during the day, especially if they have a lot of raised monuments. You might get mugged or worse!

WEAR SENSIBLE SHOES: Uneven ground makes it easy to twist an ankle in graveyards, so wear stable shoes.

MONUMENTS CAN BE DANGEROUS: Be extra cautious around large monuments. These can shift and fall without warning. This is another good reason to always visit cemeteries with another person, when possible.

DO NOT WALK ACROSS GRAVES: Avoid walking across the ground directly above the coffin, especially in older cemeteries. A wooden coffin can disintegrate over time and your weight just might be enough to cause it to cave in on itself. I spoke to someone who had this happen and he said it was quite scary. Not only did he twist his ankle, but the water table was low, so his boots quickly filled with mud, causing him to get stuck.

WATCH YOUR KIDS: Small children should be watched very carefully! Do not let them stray off designated paths. As mentioned before, monuments can shift with the earth and this could create all sorts of dangers.

CEMETERY ETIQUETTE

LEAVE MOURNERS ALONE: If you see mourners, put away your camera and notebook, and give them space. Most graveyards are large enough that you can explore a different area until other people leave.

PICNICS ARE OK: It's perfectly acceptable to enjoy a sandwich and snacks in a country graveyard. Many burial grounds are so hard to find that you may be quite hungry by the time you finally arrive.

SIT WITH CAUTION: And, yes, benches and tables at graveyards are meant to be used as such, however, be extremely cautious where you sit. Just like monuments, shifting ground can make tables and benches unstable.

BE QUIET: Just because it's OK to have a picnic, there's no need to be rowdy. And if one of you stays in the car to avoid the heat, as my husband is known to do, make sure they keep the radio volume down.

OBEY POSTED RULES: Many graveyards have a list of rules posted by the front gate. Take a moment to read these. Please don't break the rules!

KEEP PETS LEASHED: Unless the cemetery allows dogs, leave yours at home. If pets are allowed, keep them on a leash, not only as a matter of respect, but also for their safety. A falling monument can crush Fido as easily as it can crush you.

BE TIDY: Do not leave any trash, whatsoever, not even banana peels or cigarette butts. As my friend, Shelly Tucker, (fellow taphophile and the Ghost Lady of Denton, Texas) likes to say, when visiting historic graveyards, "Take only photographs and leave only footprints."

5 TYPES OF AMERICAN CEMETERIES

While you've probably noticed there are different kinds of cemeteries, it may surprise you to learn that, technically speaking, *a cemetery is not the same thing as a graveyard*. Although I've chosen to use the terms interchangeably in this book, there is a distinction. A graveyard is always connected to a church, whereas a cemetery may or may not be.

These days, the two words are commonly used interchangeably, although "graveyard" has a somewhat spooky connotation to it, while "cemetery" more mainstream. Like everything else connected to burial traditions, our words and associations with them come and go with the fashions of times.

Early American settlers, for instance, would not have used the word cemetery all. Instead, they would have chosen words such as "graveyard," "churchyard," "burying ground," and "burial ground" to describe the place where they bury their dead.

As I mentioned in Chapter 3, with the rise of the garden cemeteries of the 19th century came new terminology, and that included the word "cemetery." The word comes from the Greek word *koimeterium*, meaning "sleeping place," so it fit right in with the Victorians fondness for euphemisms such as "asleep in Jesus" and "eternal rest" for death.

Another ancient Greek word revived by the Victorians is

"necropolis." *Nekropolis* literally means "city of the dead." The word "necropolis" originally referred to a large burial site beyond city limits. Nowadays, necropolis is used mainly used by archeologists to describe ancient burial grounds. Even so, the word piqued the interest of the Victorians and can be seen on some cemetery gates from that era.

EIGHT KINDS OF US CEMETERIES

As you stroll through a historic graveyard, you may notice that it has more than one cemetery gate. Upon closer inspection, you may realize that each gate marks the entryway to different cemeteries, and that what now appears to be one big graveyard, was once two or three different ones that have merged. It's common, for instance, to see a Catholic cemetery merge with neighboring Protestant and Jewish ones, and although they once had separate names, they are now called by one single name.

Here in the United States, there are eight basic kinds of cemeteries.

1. **CHURCH CEMETERY:** A church cemetery, which is technically a graveyard, refers to a graveyard directly beside a church as well as a cemetery that is on land owned by the church, whether or not the church is immediately next door to it or not. Such graveyards are normally open to the public.

2. **PUBLIC CEMETERY:** These are owned by a city, town or county rather than being connected to a church. While they are required to be open to the public, they may have regulations to keep out vandals.

3. **PRIVATE CEMETERY:** These are owned by a corporation and are usually required to explain this affiliation with signage at the main gate. These are more expensive to be buried in than public cemeteries and church cemeteries because they are a for-profit venture. This type of cemetery often limits the type of monuments allowed in order to make maintenance cheaper. They may only allow markers that are flush to the ground and forbid flowers, for example, so they can mow more easily.

4. **MILITARY CEMETERY:** These government-operated cemeteries offer headstones and burial plots for veterans. (For more about the US Military headstones and emblems of belief, see Chapter 9.)

5. **FAMILY CEMETERY:** As the name implies, this type of cemetery is family-owned. It may simply be a designated area on family-owned land where family members and perhaps a few close friends are buried. At one time, there were thousands of such graveyards in the United States. While family cemeteries are still legal in most states, they are no longer common.

6. **CUSTOMARY CEMETERY:** This is the least official type of cemetery. Rather than being owned by a particular family, corporation, church or other group, it is simply a place where a group of neighbors or some other group started burying people because it was convenient to them.

Like family cemeteries, this type of cemetery was much more common in rural areas during the early settlers. This type of cemetery is the most easily overlooked and forgotten and can be frustrating for genealogists and researchers, since they often lack accurate burial records due to the informal arrangement.

7. MASS GRAVE: After a natural disaster or large scale accident, victims may be buried together in a single gravesite. Often, a memorial is erected in their honor.

8. LODGE CEMETERY: These cemeteries are owned and operated by fraternal groups or other clubs, such as the Oddfellows, Elks, or Masons. Although you may assume otherwise, these cemeteries often allow non-members to be buried there, as well.

6 NAMES, DATES & EPITAPHS

The simple act of strolling through historic graveyards reading the names and epitaphs on the markers can be quite entertaining. Popular names change over the decades, and some are so unique that you only see them once. For example, here in Texas, I came across the grave for a woman named "Thlitha." Not only is that name unique, but I am still not certain how to pronounce it!

Even if you are not related to the deceased, you may find certain graves so intriguing that you want to know more. These days, with search engines like Google and genealogy resources such as Ancestry.com, you can often satisfy the curiosity inspired by your visit to a historic graveyard with a few simple computer keystrokes.

NAMING TRADITIONS OF THE PAST

Our ancestors often followed a traditional naming sequence that differs from today and was based on the fact that back then, large families were the norm. These days, for instance, the first born is more likely to bear the name of his mother or father, but in the past, this didn't happen until the third child. Of course, just like today, there were always exceptions to the rule.

NAMES FOR BOYS

In the past, American families often followed this naming tradition for their sons:

Firstborn son: Father's father.
Second son: Mother's father.
Third son: Father, a.k.a. 'Junior.'
Fourth son: Father's oldest brother.
Fifth son: Mother's oldest brother (or father's second oldest brother.)

NAMES FOR GIRLS

This naming tradition followed a similar logic for little girls:

Firstborn daughter: Mother's mother.
Second daughter: Father's mother.
Third daughter: Mother
Fourth daughter: Mother's oldest sister.
Fifth daughter: Father's oldest sister (or mother's second oldest sister.)

UNNAMED INFANTS

As I mention in Chapter 9, in the United States, unknown soldiers were originally buried with headstones engraved with numbers only. No dates or other information was added.

Here in Texas, I came across another usage for numbers instead of names on graves. Known locally as "the lost cemetery of infants," the graveyard attached to the Berachah Industrial Home for the Redemption and Protection of Erring Girls is a burial ground where unwed mothers buried their illegitimate children during the late 1800's through the early 1900's. (Babies who survived were put up for adoption.)

For the babies too young to have been named, the markers bear only a number, such as "Infant 46." Other markers simply display a first name. Omitting the last name was a courtesy meant to protect the unwed mother's anonymity. This way, after learning a skill at the school, she could reenter society without having to share her secret with anyone. Her reputation would remain unsullied.

DATES ON HEADSTONES:

Generally speaking, headstones will have the birth date and death date of the deceased inscribed on the front. There are a couple of exceptions you may run across in historic cemeteries.

DOUBLE DATING IN HISTORIC GRAVEYARDS:

As genealogists already know, there's nothing romantic about the term "double dating" when it comes to historic research. Double dating occurs when you see a person with two different birth or death dates engraved on their headstone.

It all started in 1582, when Pope Gregor XIII decided to make the year start in January, rather than in March, as it previously had. While this may sound arbitrary, the pope had legitimate reasons for these changes. Pope Julian's calendar, also called the "Old Style calendar" required constant adjustments so that important dates such as the Spring Equinox and the Summer Solstice, dates which correspond to specific astronomical events each year, would fall on the correct date.

Easter, for instance, is celebrated on the first Sunday after the first full moon that occurs on or after the Spring Equinox. So the pope was merely trying to make the calendar year more accurate, and while it made things confusing for a while, the end results were worth it. We now only require a Leap Year once every four years, instead of making constant adjustments to our calendar each year thanks to the Gregorian calendar.

Unfortunately, the only way to make this new calendar work at first was to *delete* 11 days from the calendar year. However, by the time the American colonies had adopted the Gregorian calendar in 1752, things had shifted enough that people now needed to *add* 11 days to the year. Because of all this, some early American headstones feature more than one date of birth and death for the deceased. Such double dating is found most commonly throughout New England on graves from the mid to late 1700's.

Confused, yet? You are not alone. Despite the confusion, people often changed their birthdates to reflect the Gregorian calendar. George Washington, for instance, changed his birthdate from February 11, 1732 (based on the Old Style calendar) to February 22, 1732 to reflect the Gregorian calendar system.

Thomas Jefferson, on the other hand, chose to keep his original birthdate on his tombstone, so it reads "April 2, 1743 O.S." The "O.S." after his birthdate stands for "Old Style."

THE HEBREW CALENDAR

Confusing dates may also be found in historic Jewish cemeteries. You may, for instance, see a headstone with an impossible-sounding birthdate such as March 4, 5649. This is because the traditional Jewish calendar begins 3,760 years before the Christian one. To figure out the date as it applies to the Gregorian calendar, you need to subtract 3760 from it. In the example I just gave, 5649 minus 3760 lets you know that the person was born in 1889.

EPITAPHS

Epitaphs are the words of remembrance inscribed on a grave marker. The practice of using epitaphs dates back to ancient Greece. The word "epitaph" comes from the Greek *epi,* meaning "around" and *taph* meaning "tomb."

RIP

Perhaps the most well-known epitaph of all is RIP, an easy-to-remember acronym for the Latin phrase *Resquiat in Pace*, meaning "Rest in Peace." In Roman days, however, *Sta viator*, meaning "Pause, traveler" was more commonly used, since Roman soldiers were often buried by the roadside.

EARLY COLONIAL EPITAPHS

In America, generally speaking, the older the epitaph, the grimmer it will sound and the less personal it will be. Puritans, for instance, often used the phrase *Memento Mori* on their headstones, Latin for "Remember you must die."

Gravestones for colonial era Americans rarely included more than the birth and death date. For the most part, epitaphs were reserved for prestigious men, and rarely bestowed on the graves of women.

Gradually, epitaphs began to shift in tone from dire reminders to die, to gentler sounding phrases such as,

"Here lies the mortal remains of..." to "Sacred to the memory of..." and "Gone, but not forgotten." Some of the most poetic, uplifting and personal epitaphs arose with the popularity of America's garden cemeteries.

MODERN EPITAPHS

Nowadays, epitaphs can be formulaic or highly personal. They run the gamut from brief phrases, poems, song lyrics and scriptures, to a lengthy list of of the deceased's attributes. I recently came across a modern one that read more like a Linked In profile than an epitaph!

What I enjoy about epitaphs is how much personality, and even humor, they add to a graveyard visit. One of my favorites can be seen in Key West, Florida on the grave of a woman who caught flack for being a hypochondriac. After she passed away in 1979, B.P. "Pearl" Roberts used her epitaph to sum up a lifetime of frustration with one little phrase, "I told you I was sick."

In the same cemetery, I also saw headstones reading "Just resting my eyes," "Devoted fan of singer Julio Iglesias," and, "If you're reading this, you desperately need a hobby." I'm not sure what it is about "Margaritaville" that inspires these one-liners, but I have never seen so many humorous epitaphs in a single graveyard.

7 STICKS & STONES

L ike epitaphs and symbols, the materials used for American burial markers have evolved through our nation's history. This chapter gives a brief overview of the most common materials used for cemetery monuments in the United States.

FIELD STONES & CAIRNS

One of the the simplest ways to mark a burial is to leave a pile of stones on the grave. This practice is common around the world and throughout history, including the United States.

A pile of rocks used to mark a grave is called a "cairn." A single stone is called a "field stone." Certain Native American tribes used cairns to mark their burial sites, and even today, people sometimes incorporate a stone from their family's property into their monument.

WOODEN GRAVE MARKERS

Wood was also used for burial markers by the earliest Americans. Throughout the Southwest and Florida, early Spanish missionaries often used simple wooden crosses to mark graves. (Although any Native Americans they happened to convert to Christianity were simply wrapped in shrouds or blankets and buried without a coffin or marker.)

Wood grave marker in Thurber Cemetery Thurber, TX

POST AND RAIL

Even today, post and rail fences dot the scenery as you take a scenic country drive in America. Post and rail style burial markers were a common (and affordable) option for early settlers. These were made by laying one or two pieces of wood horizontally on top of two vertical posts. Unfortunately, due to the transient properties of wood, few of these remain.

BOIS D'ARC WOOD

Wooden markers continued to be used and were especially common in impoverished areas right through the 20th Century. The problem with wooden markers is that unless they are tended, painted, repaired or otherwise maintained, they eventually rot and disappear into the earth.

Here in Texas, the most enduring of these wooden burial markers are made from bois d'arc, a tree which has special properties that prevent it from rotting as quickly as other wood.

Left: White bronze monument in Weatherford, TX
Right: Close up of detachable panels people ordered
from a catalog to customize these monuments.

ENGRAVED STONES

When early Americans engraved stone markers, they
relied mainly on native stones, such as slate and sandstone.
It wasn't until the railroads became established that people
could more easily transport marble, limestone and granite.

For many years, marble was considered the most upscale
choice for creating cemetery monuments, since only
wealthy families could afford to have this beautiful white
stone imported and engraved. The problem with marble,
and with limestone, as well, is that both of these stones
become worn. Within a few decades, the inscriptions on
these headstones becomes difficult to read. Granite,
however, remains a popular choice for cemetery

monuments even today because it is much more durable..

HOLLOW ZINC A.K.A. 'WHITE BRONZE'

From 1874 to 1914, the Monumental Bronze Company of Bridgeport Connecticut offered custom-made monuments made from a zinc alloy. Called "white bronze" to make them sound fancier, not only were these metal monuments less expensive than carved marble or limestone, but they were also much more durable. In fact, the inscriptions on these monuments are clearly legible even today. People could order these monuments through a catalogue, and customize them accordingly.

After you've seen a few examples in person, you'll be able to easily recognize white bronze monuments by their distinctive bluish gray color. If you're not sure though, simply give one a tap with a stick or your hand. Since these are hollow constructions, you will hear a metallic ringing sound. During the Prohibition Era, it's claimed that bootleggers sometimes pried panels off of these since monuments to hide booze inside.

During World War One, zinc was needed for guns and munitions, so the Monumental Bronze Company shifted its focus to aid the war effort. In 1939, they went out of business completely.

GRANITE MONUMENTS

Cemetery monument builders began using granite in the 1860's and it remains popular to this day. Unlike marble and limestone, granite weathers well, so inscriptions remain legible as the years pass. In fact, granite is one of the hardest substances known to man. On the Mohs scale, it ranks as a 7. (Just for comparison, marble rates from 3-5 on the Mohs hardness scale, while diamonds rank 10.)

OTHER MATERIALS

While granite remains the most popular substance for creating modern cemetery monuments, you may still come across grave markers made from other materials ranging from marbles, cement, and even PVC piping. Often these alternative materials are born from economic necessity, but even so, they can often be just as beautiful and interesting as grand stone monuments.

8 COINS PEBBLES & SEASHELLS

Whe hen people visit graves, they often leave items at the gravesite such as coins, pebbles, seashells, decorations and items called "grave goods."

GRAVE GOODS VS GRAVE DECORATIONS

Items left at a gravesite that once belonged to the deceased or that are associated with the deceased, are called "grave goods." Grave goods may be left on top of the gravesite or buried with the deceased. The famous rocker, Dimebag Darrell, offers a good example for both types of grave goods. Not only is he buried with one of Eddie Van Halen's guitars, but visitors often leave little bottles of booze on his grave as a tribute to his hard-partying rock and roll lifestyle.

Grave decorations, on the other hand, are simply items meant to beautify a gravesite. In modern graveyards, I often see solar powered lights, colorful pinwheels and wind chimes as grave decorations.

GRAVE GOODS WERE A COMMON SIGHT

Up until the 1930's grave goods were a common sight throughout the US no matter which ethnicity, background or religious beliefs were involved, except for Jewish people

Grave goods: Dimebag Darrell is buried with one of
Eddie Van Halen's guitars in Arlington, TX

(more on this below.) Americans of all racial and ethnic
backgrounds frequently left household items and toys at
gravesites. In some communities, these items were often
intentionally broken before being placed on a grave. This
sometimes led to the misconception that mourners were
using the family grave as a trash heap, when it was actually
a symbolic gesture on their part.

After the Great Depression, perpetual care became the
norm for modern American cemeteries. Cemetery
organizations became much more strict about the types of
grave goods they will allow. Even so, the practice continues
to this day.

MEXICAN AMERICAN GRAVE GOODS

Mexican Americans have unique cultural traditions surrounding their use of grave goods. Although they may leave items at grave sites throughout the year, its especially noticeable during the *Dia de los Muertos,* a.k.a. "Day of the Dead," a celebration that combines beliefs from Mayan, Aztec, and Catholic traditions.

The bulk of Mexican American Day of the Dead festivities take place on All Hallows Eve (October 31), All Saints Day (November 1), and All Souls Eve (November 2), although celebrations may continue through mid-November.

While respectful, these celebrations are not sorrowful. It is meant as a celebration. During this time, families gather in the cemetery to clean the graves of their ancestors and to decorate them with offerings called *offerendas*, which may include candles, favorite food items, sugar skulls, candy skeletons, bottles of booze, and other items.

Bright orange Mexican marigolds feature prominently in Day of the Dead floral arrangements. This is because of a belief that spirits are attracted to the distinct odor of marigolds and will use its scent to guide them to the land of the living and back again.

In addition to the Days of the Dead, Mexican Americans may also visit grave sites throughout the year to commemorate birthdays and other special occasions.

Mexican American grave markers may also contain special niches called *nichos*. Nichos symbolize labyrinthine caves the Mesoamericans believed the soul must journey through during the afterlife. Offerings left inside these nichos are meant to facilitate the deceased's journey and appease any entities they encounter along the way.

Grave goods: Pantera fans leave booze bottles & guitar picks as tributes to Dimebag Darrell.

ASIAN AMERICAN GRAVE GOODS

Many Asian cultures designate special times of year for cleaning and maintaining their ancestor's graves. Some also place food and flowers as offerings. They may also burn incense and money (not real money, but paper meant to symbolize money) at the grave.

In China and Korea, April 5th is a holiday called Qingming, which means "tomb sweeping day." In addition to visiting graves on birthdays, many Asian cultures have special rituals associated with the anniversary of the deceased's death.

ROMANI AMERICAN GRAVE GOODS

Romani Americans, sometimes called "gypsies" or "travelers," are so close knit and not integrated into mainstream society that the average US citizen is unaware of their existence. For this reason, they are often called the "hidden Americans," and their population is estimated to be one million.

Here in Texas, Romani Americans may picnic at a gravesite.When they drink soda, beer or liquor at the grave of a loved one, they often leave the empty cans and bottles behind as grave goods.

PEBBLES ON JEWISH GRAVES

Grave goods are not a common practice in Jewish cemeteries, however, small pebbles are often left on graves by visiting friends and family members. For Jews and Christians, alike, leaving stones at a grave is a nod to Genesis 13:19-20, in which Jacob erects a pillar at Rachel's gravesite. By leaving a pebble at a grave, it symbolizes building a pillar in your loved one's honor.

COINS ON GRAVES

The practice of leaving coins with the deceased dates back to the ancient Greeks, who believed the rivers Styx and Acheron separated the living from the dead. A ferry trip was required to cross these waters, otherwise the soul of the deceased would be forced to wander the river banks for 100 years. To avoid this, ancient Greeks placed a coin in the mouths of their dead as a way to pay the Charon, as this ancient ferryman was called.

These days, coins may be found on just about anyone's grave, but I see them most often on the graves of historic figures, especially criminals, such as the notorious "Machine Gun Kelley."

Perhaps, even now, we worry that criminals and outcasts may need assistance in the afterlife. That said, the main purpose for leaving coins on a grave simply appears to be a way of letting others know this person is still remembered.

Coins on graves: Machine Gun Kelley in Paradise, TX

COINS ON MILITARY GRAVES

A modern urban legend that first began making the rounds of the internet around 2009 claims that when coins are seen on military headstones, the different denominations mean specific things. A quarter, for instance, allegedly means you served in the same unit as the deceased, or (according to another online source) a quarter means that you were present when the deceased lost his life.

While researching this book, however, I was unable to find any reference to the origins of this practice. I finally turned to snopes.com, a website that specializes in alerting people to urban legends. Turns out that this is a modern myth.

Of course, you still may find coins on a military

headstone, just as you may find them on *anybody's* headstone. I merely wanted to clarify that the practice of having different coins to signify specific things on military headstones is a recent idea and not a longstanding practice.

That said, grave goods ranging from stuffed animals and photographs to military medals and coins frequently appear in American military cemeteries. There is even something called a "challenge coin" that may be left by military personnel on a headstone.

Challenge coins are non-monetary metal tokens that some military units provide in order to promote morale. These tokens may be inscribed with a soldier's unit or other identifying information. Like other grave goods, a challenge coin may be left on a military headstone.

In 2009, the US Army Center of Military history began archiving grave goods left in military cemeteries. Curators now keep track of which headstone the items were left upon. Also, if the family members would like those items, which range from stuffed animals and photographs to medals and coins, they are welcome to have them. Prior to that, these grave goods often wound up in the garbage.

SEASHELLS ON GRAVES

Graves adorned with seashells are fairly common in historic graveyards throughout the south, and not just in coastal regions as you might expect. This practice extends quite far inland; I've seen quite a few in the rural graveyards of north Texas.

One of the most challenging items I researched for this book was the symbolic meaning of seashells on American graves. It is difficult to pinpoint the exact symbolic meaning and cultural origins for this practice.

AN ANCIENT TRADITION

Decorating graves with seashells is such an ancient custom that it even pre-dates the ancient Egyptians! Of all the burial practices I researched for this book, decorating graves with seashells appears to be the most primal.

Mounded cement grave with seashells pressed into it.

GREEK AND ROMAN ORIGINS

To the ancient Greeks and Romans, seashells were a symbol of the divine feminine. Venus, the Roman goddess of love and fertility, was said to have been birthed by sea foam and carried to the show on a scallop shell.

CHRISTIAN ORIGINS

Over time, these Greek and Roman beliefs seeped into Christianity. Some believe that Mother Mary herself is a nod to how the oceans gave birth to life, and point out that her name comes from the Latin word *mare,* meaning "sea."

In addition to the connection with the Virgin Mary, seashells are a symbolic reference to religious pilgrimages. This is because during the Middle Ages, pilgrims often sewed scallop shells into their garments as they traveled and used seashells to mark the pathways for others to follow.

In Christianity, seashells also symbolize spiritual protection and are associated with baptism. In Catholic churches, the tool used to sprinkle water on the heads of babies during their baptism is often shaped like a scallop shell.

AFRICAN AMERICAN ORIGINS

African Americans who decorated their graves with seashells may have carried this practice to America from their ancestors rather than taking the idea from Christianity.

Historians point out that African tribes from the Congo region often apply seashells to mounded dirt graves. According to their beliefs, the spirit world was a brightly lit place, and dead people became gleaming white creatures who lived beneath rivers and lakes. Covering graves in bleached white shells was considered a way to help the deceased blend into the bright white world of the afterlife.

SEASHELLS AS GRAVE GOODS

Sometimes, rather than being part of the monument itself, seashells are left on a grave. Specifically, conch shells and whelks are frequently seen in historic cemeteries. I've been told by several people that this means a loved one made a pilgrimage to the deceased's grave, leaving a shell behind as a reminder of their visit.

Even so, I am still not 100% convinced. As sociologists and historians are well aware, people often continue a tradition even after the original intent behind it is forgotten. Once the original intent is forgotten, people will simply guess as to why they are doing it. That's how urban legends are born.

Symbolically, however, the spiral shape of a conch shell represents the challenging spiral path of life and death.

Seashells on graves: Visitors leave seashells on this sea captain's grave in Old Biloxi Cemetery in Biloxi, MS

9 AMERICAN HEADSTONE STYLES

Until the 1500's, gravestones were mainly for the rich and powerful. If you weren't clergy, royalty, rich, or some other notable figure, you weren't going to get a fancy burial, let alone an engraved marker to commemorate your life. If your gravesite was marked in anyway, it would be with wood or stones as described in the previous chapter.

So when the first European explorers arrived on America's shores, headstones for common folk was still a relatively new idea. It took a shift in the religious mindset to make headstones an acceptable practice. Even then, some religious sects felt headstones were an unnecessary testament to human vanity. The Quakers, for instance, did not officially approve the use of headstones until 1850.

Despite lacking a monarchy, American headstones are a reflection of a person's wealth and stature in life, and not simply their religious beliefs. Many early American settlers were placed in unmarked graves, not due to any aversion to the practice, but simply because they could not afford a tombstone.

WHY MANY HEADSTONES FACE EAST

As the name suggests, a headstone marks where the head of the deceased is situated. In most Christian cemeteries, burials are oriented so that the headstone faces east. This tradition ensures that people will be facing the right direction when the sun comes up on Judgment Day. In the old days, ministers sometimes chose to be buried facing west so that they could be facing their flock on that day of awakening.

European churchyards had a strict pecking order when it came to which side of the church you were buried on. For instance, just as the best side of the church to be buried on was the east, the worst side was the north. The north was where bastards, criminals and strangers were buried. Suicides were sometimes buried on the north side of a church yard, however, in the Middle Ages, they were not allowed to enter through the church yard gates. Their bodies were, instead, passed over the north wall.

Like so many other American burial customs, beliefs about headstone directions migrated here with European settlers and reflects their Christian beliefs. Pay attention to the direction that a headstone is facing when you visit historic graveyards in America.

Check to see if there are any graves outside of the main gates or off by themselves. You may find suicides, slaves, criminals, people who were ostracized in life, or who simply did not belong to any of the local religions buried off by themselves.

In Eastland, Texas, for instance, the postmistress Marene Johnson-Johnson chose to be buried at a perpendicular to her husband's feet out of a belief that just as she had served him in life, she wanted to serve him in death!

So while there is not a hard and fast rule here in the United States regarding burial direction, if you notice a grave facing a different direction than all the rest, you may discover an interesting story behind it.

Traditional burial position: Wife on the left.

Exceptions: More common on older stones

CEMETERY LAYOUT

Many historic cemeteries are divided into family plots, but that is not always the case. Graveyards established by German immigrants often arrange their gravesites in a very linear and orderly fashion. In these burial grounds you may find only the husband and wife beside each other while the rest of the family are buried elsewhere. Some graveyards may bury children separately from adults.

LEFT AND RIGHT ON HEADSTONES

Married folks often share a headstone, and when they do, most of the time you will notice that – as you stand facing the monument – the wife's *name* will be on the right, and the husband's *name* will be on the left.

If you've ever attended a traditional Christian wedding, then you may also recall that the bride's family sits on the left side of the church and the groom's on the right. So when you approach a headstone, you are essentially standing where the minister would be standing while conducting the wedding ceremony.

The reasons for having the woman on the left and men on the right have grown murky over time. One school of thought claims the reason a bride stands to the left of her husband is so that she is closest to his heart, and maybe that's true. It's certainly a romantic notion!

Another idea is that grooms kept their brides on the left in order to keep their fighting arm free to swing a sword if needed during the ceremony. This supposedly hearkens back to the days when brides were sometimes snatched away by competitors, even in the middle of a marriage ceremony.

VEIN OF LOVE

While attempting to sort out all of this right/left symbolism, I learned that the ancient Romans believed a special vein ran from the fourth finger of the left hand directly up the arm and straight to the heart. This vein was called the "vena amoris," which means "vein of love" in Latin. This is the origin for wearing our wedding bands on that finger. And, hey, maybe the ancients were onto something here. After all, a common heart attack symptom for men includes pain radiating down the left arm.

In any case, it has become traditional for wives to be buried on the left, with their husbands buried on the right. Just like everything else, there are exceptions to this rule.

German immigrants, for instance, often place the husband's body on the left and the wife's on the right.

Footstones: Often reveal family nicknames

FOOTSTONES

Family plots often feature one large monument around which the other relatives are buried. While this monument may have the names of family members inscribed on it, it usually only has the family's last name. So, you might see a large marker that simply reads, "Smith."

Other family members will be buried in the family plot, with smaller headstones indicating their full names, birth and death dates. Family plots such as these often include foot stones. Just as a headstone is placed at the head of the deceased, a foot stone is placed at their feet.

If you are researching a person, foot stones can provide valuable information since they are most often engraved with a family title, such as "mother, " and "brother," or even a nickname, such as "Nunny."

WHY HEADSTONES HAVE ROUNDED TOPS

America's earliest carved stone grave markers were erected by the Puritans in New England. It's no accident that these headstones look much like ones in England's historic graveyards. Their distinctive design was not based on an artistic whim, but is meant to imitate the shape of the stone tablets upon which Moses received the Ten Commandments in the Bible's Old Testament.

The rounded top of these markers is called the "lunette" or "tympanum." The thin borders along the side are called "pilasters." The middle part, where the name, date and epitaph go is called the "ledger." The rounded tops of the borders are the headstone's "shoulders" or "finials."

SQUARED OFF TOPS

Over time, American headstones became more streamlined in appearance. This was likely due to a combination of fashion and practicality. Rectangles are easier to create than rounded tops.

US MILITARY HEADSTONES

US Military headstones are a formalized style of grave marker, although their design has been modified over the years. The first official military headstone designs were adopted by the US War Department in 1873. These marble markers are 4 inches thick and 10 inches wide. As for height, regulations require the above-ground portion to stand 12 inches high.

When you visit historic graveyards, you may notice that these monuments often stand taller than 12 inches. So just because the original regulations say 12 inches, doesn't mean that's how you will find them. Why? I'm not sure, but it's important to keep in mind that many of these headstones have shifted or even fallen over over time, so they have been re-situated.

CIVIL WAR TYPE

Civil War Type headstones are decorated with a carved image of a shield which usually contains the soldier's name, rank, and home state inscribed inside it in bas relief. The above ground marble portion is polished and has a slight curve along the top side. This original US military headstone is commonly referred to as the "Civil War Type." Originally, there were available *only* for Union soldiers.

NOT JUST FOR CIVIL WAR SOLDIERS

Although it's called the Civil War Type, this style of headstone was also used to mark the graves of soldiers from the the Mexican War, Indian Campaigns, the War of 1812, the Spanish-American War, and even the American Revolution.

CONFEDERATE SOLDIERS

It wasn't until 1906 that Congress passed a law to provide official military headstones for Confederate soldiers. Even so, these headstones differ slightly from other Civil War style markers; the tops come to a point rather than being rounded, and the shield design is omitted entirely.

More than one historian has told me that the reason Confederate soldier's monuments are pointed is, "to keep those damn Yankees from sitting on it."

GENERAL TYPE - STILL USED TODAY

Shortly after WWI, a new design was created for US military markers. Called "the General Type" because the committee which created it included two generals (General John. J. Pershing and Quartermaster General Harry L. Rogers) this style of military marker remains in use to this day.

The General Type is a military headstone 4 inches thick and 13 inches wide, with the above ground portion measuring 42 inches tall. As always, the above ground height will vary in the real world. I have even seen headstones of the only General Type of US military headstone flush to the ground.

US MILITARY EMBLEMS OF BELIEF

The tablet of a US military General Type marker is inscribed with the soldier's name, rank, regiment, division, date of death and home state. In addition, the General type of military marker allows space for a religious emblem. At first the only choices were a Latin Cross for Christians and a Star of David for Judaism. This has really expanded, however, and now includes emblems for atheists and as of 2013, those who identify as pagans or Odinists, may evens use Thor's Hammer.

OTHER MILITARY MARKERS

It should be noted that veterans are not required to use official military headstone markers. They are provided upon request out of courtesy and respect. So when you visit a historic graveyard, don't assume that the only veterans are the ones with official government headstones.

Watch for cemetery symbols that will let you know that a person served in the military, such as crossed cannons, shields, and military unit emblems. It's beyond the scope of this book to include every single emblem for every single military unit, but if you see one, take a photo and you may be able to track it down on the internet.

UNKNOWN SOLDIERS - OLD & NEW

At first, the monuments for unknown soldiers differed from those whose name and rank were known. If you find a numbered cube in a historic graveyard, there's a good chance that it is one of these original Civil War type markers for an unknown soldier.

These headstones are marble cut 6 inches on all sides and then 30 inches long. The top of this and the first 4 inches of each side are polished. Use of this numbered cube style of headstone for unknown soldiers was gradually phased out. Unknown soldiers now receive the exact same style of headstone as for those who are known.

I am grateful to the US Department of Veterans Affairs for granting me permission to share the following:

U.S. Department of Veterans Affairs

National Cemetery Administration

AVAILABLE EMBLEMS OF BELIEF FOR PLACEMENT ON GOVERNMENT HEADSTONES AND MARKERS

(1) LATIN (CHRISTIAN) CROSS | (2) BUDDHIST | (3) JUDAISM (Star of David) | (4) PRESBYTERIAN CROSS | (5) RUSSIAN ORTHODOX CROSS | (6) LUTHERAN CROSS | (7) EPISCOPAL CROSS | (8) UNITARIAN (Flaming Chalice)

(9) UNITED METHODIST | (10) AARONIC ORDER CHURCH | (11) MORMON (Angel Moroni) | (12) NATIVE AMERICAN CHURCH OF NORTH AMERICA | (13) SERBIAN ORTHODOX | (14) GREEK CROSS | (15) BAHAI (9-Pointed Star)

(16) ATHEIST | (17) MUSLIM (Crescent and Star) | (18) HINDU | (19) KONKO-KYO FAITH | (20) COMMUNITY OF CHRIST | (21) SUFISM REORIENTED | (22) TENRIKYO CHURCH

(23) SEICHO-NO-IE | (24) THE CHURCH OF WORLD MESSIANITY | (25) UNITED CHURCH OF RELIGIOUS SCIENCE | (26) CHRISTIAN REFORMED CHURCH | (27) UNITED MORAVIAN CHURCH | (28) ECKANKAR | (29) CHRISTIAN CHURCH

(30) CHRISTIAN & MISSIONARY ALLIANCE | (31) UNITED CHURCH OF CHRIST | (32) HUMANIST EMBLEM OF SPIRIT | (33) PRESBYTERIAN CHURCH (USA) | (34) IZUMO TAISHAKYO MISSION OF HAWAII | (35) SOKA GAKKAI INTERNATIONAL (USA) | (36) SIKH (KHANDA) | (37) WICCA (Pentacle)

(38) LUTHERAN CHURCH MISSOURI SYNOD (39) NEW APOSTOLIC (40) SEVENTH DAY ADVENTIST CHURCH (41) CELTIC CROSS (42) ARMENIAN CROSS (43) FAROHAR (44) MESSIANIC JEWISH

(45) KOHEN HANDS (46) CATHOLIC CELTIC CROSS (47) FIRST CHURCH OF CHRIST, SCIENTIST (Cross & Crown) (48) MEDICINE WHEEL (49) INFINITY (51) LUTHER ROSE (52) LANDING EAGLE

(53) FOUR DIRECTIONS (54) CHURCH OF NAZARENE (55) HAMMER OF THOR (56) UNIFICATION CHURCH (57) SANDHILL CRANE (58) CHURCH OF GOD (59) POMEGRANATE

(60) MESSIANIC (61) Shinto (62) Sacred Heart (63) African Ancestral Traditionalist (64) Maltese Cross (65) Druid (Awen)

10 MONUMENTS & OTHER STRUCTURES

Headstones are only the beginning. Most historic cemeteries also feature different types of monuments, along with other structures including tabernacles, mausoleums, spirit houses, and more.

CEMETERY GATES

The first thing to catch your eye as you approach a cemetery is its gate, if it has one. From a practical standpoint, gates protect burial grounds from grazing livestock, however even they have a deeper meaning. Cemetery gates are most often made of iron, and they are usually painted black.

Iron is used for cemetery gates not so much for symbolic reasons, as for a longstanding superstition that iron repels spirits. Cemetery gates are often topped with black spiked iron. This is a nod to medieval hearses. In this context, however, a hearse has nothing to do with a funeral carriage or car. In the Middle Ages, a hearse was the spiked iron gate placed above a castle's drawbridge to protect this most vulnerable area from attack. While a spiked fence may discourage human intruders, it's also meant to discourage restless souls. Surrounding a burial ground with an iron gate, then, is meant to keep the spirits of the deceased contained within it.

Painting cemetery gates black dates to an ancient belief that when people died, the beginning of their journey took place in utter darkness. Only by wearing black would they blend in and be protected from evil spirits during the first part of their soul's journey.

This is also why black is associated with funerals, hearses (now I'm talking about funeral carriages and cars) and mourning apparel.

LICHGATES

A lichgate gets its name from the word *lych,* an Old English word for "corpse." This Saxon word makes its way into several words relating to funeral lore: A lych bell was the handbell rung by the person leading a funeral procession as they carried the deceased along a lych path, the road leading to the burial site. It could be worrisome if along the way they heard a lych owl (another name for a "screech owl") because its cry was said to portend death.

Although some people call any cemetery entrance a lichgate, it's traditional for lichgates to be covered by a roof. In the Middle Ages on up through the Victorian Era, the dead were wrapped in cloth, placed on a bier, then taken to the lichgate until the funeral. Not only did the lichgate keep rain off of mourners, but it often had benches along the side for them to rest upon as they waited for the minister to arrive.

Even today, in some parts of the deep south, the funeral party waits outside the cemetery gates until the minister requests permission from the heavens for the deceased to enter.

OPEN AIR PAVILIONS A.K.A. TABERNACLES:

In America, lichgates are not as common as open-air shelters called tabernacles, especially in rural cemeteries. Tabernacles often have benches and a pulpit. Like lichgates, tabernacles offer shelter during funerals. Tabernacles are also useful during annual cemetery cleanups and other gatherings.

Cemetery gates   Gated family plot

GATED CEMETERY PLOTS

For the reasons stated earlier in this chapter, these, too, are most often made of pointed iron that is painted black. Gated cemetery plots serve practical functions, as well, by making it clear exactly which area a family is required to tend, along with keeping livestock out of the area.

THE GATES AJAR

In 1868, Elizabeth Stuart Phelps published a book entitled *The Gates Ajar*. She tells the story of a young woman grieving the loss of her brother, a soldier who died in the Civil War. After his death, our heroine is unable to accept the senselessness of his death. She even finds her faith challenged as she questions the actions of God.

She eventually finds solace by embracing ideas passed

from her aunt, who tells her that the gates to heaven are not closed, but ajar. Since these gates do not close behind the dead, departed souls are able to pass back and forth between Heaven and earth. In this way, loved ones who have passed away are able to observe friends and family members who are still among the living.

Heavenly Gates: The Gates Ajar

In addition, the afterlife that Phelps describes in her books is a very pleasant place, where people remain in their human form and go about the same activities as they did in life, even playing the piano, for example.

As mentioned earlier, after the tremendous loss of lives during the Civil War, America was a nation in mourning. This was also a time when many Christians believed that God had already decided who would go to Heaven and who would go to Hell, regardless of their behavior while alive. Needless to say, there were many Americans who could relate to the conflicts in Phelps' book.

Critics of *The Gates Ajar* denounced it as misguided at best and heretical at worst. Despite all this controversy, Phelps' book was wildly successful. In fact, *The Gates Ajar* was so popular that it triggered one of America's first mass-marketing campaigns, including Gates Ajar clothing, cigars, patent medicines, and numerous songs, with titles such as "Gates Ajar," "the Gate Ajar for Me," "Passed within the Gates Ajar," and many more.

By the 1880's, florists began creating special flower arrangements in an arch shape to represent the famous gates ajar from Phelp's book. Even today, a quick Google search for florists and the keywords "gates ajar" shows that the flower arrangement named after Phelps' book remains an enduring tradition.

When you see monuments in cemeteries from 1868 and on, look for epitaphs referencing "gates ajar." Many times when you see engravings of heavenly gates with the doors ajar, it is a reference to a controversial book that comforted a grieving nation in the late 1800's.

MAUSOLEUM

The word "mausoleum" comes from the Greek word *Mausoleion* which is what they called the opulent marble tomb we know as Halicarnassus, and that was one of the original Seven Wonders of the Ancient World. Over time, the word "mausoleum" came to represent any grand tomb.

In modern conversation, a mausoleum is a stand-alone, external building containing interment space for several coffins. They are usually built for a specific family. Mausoleums tend to be reserved for the wealthiest of families, those who, like ancient royalty, can afford to build magnificent tombs for themselves.

CENOTAPH

When a monument or mausoleum lacks bodies, it is called a *cenotaph*. The Greek roots of this word are *kenos* for empty and *taphos* for tomb. Cenotaphs are often built to honor a notable person or group, even though the people, themselves, are buried elsewhere.

A cenotaph can be fancy or simple, like this.

COLUMBARIUM

A columbarium is a burial structure containing niches to place the urns of cremated people, or cremains as they are called in polite society. The word "columbarium" comes from the Latin word *columbarius* meaning "dove cote," and refers to how the niches in a columbarium look like the nesting boxes for doves.

Columbarium in Greenwood Memorial Park, Ft Worth, TX

SARCOPHAGUS

The word "sarcophagus" comes from the Greek *sarkophagos,* which literally means "flesh eating." This is because the earliest stone crypts were made from Assius stone, a rock so caustic that in a few short weeks, a body placed within a sarcophagus made from it was reduced to nothing but bone.

While sarcophagi were originally meant to hold a body, they are often decorative especially here in America. One notable exception I have come across is in San Antonio, Texas.

Ashes of the Alamo dead in a hip tomb style sarcophagus

After the infamous siege in 1835, the bodies of the Alamo defenders including Jim Bowie, Davy Crockett, and William B. Travis were not buried.

Instead, Mexican general, Santa Anna, ordered their bodies to be drenched with oil and burned to a crisp. In an era when many people truly believed that they would need their body intact when Judgment Day came, this cremation was a clear sign of disrespect. Eventually, these cremains were shoveled into a coffin and secretly buried beneath the altar in a local church.

One hundred years later, while remodeling the church, workers stumbled onto a dilapidated coffin full of ashes.

These ashes were placed in a sarcophagus and put on public display.

SARCOPHAGUS VARIATIONS:
Generally speaking, a sarcophagus is a large rectangular container made of stone or concrete. It may contain either the body or the coffin of the deceased, or it may simply be ornamental, with the body buried beneath.There are many types of sarcophagi, including:

CHEST OR BOX TOMB: A chest tomb, also called a box tomb, is the most plain-looking sarcophagus variation you will see. It looks like a big coffin shaped box on the ground, and is minimally decorated.

Box (a.k.a. Chest) tombs are plain rectangles

ALTAR TOMB: This is like a chest tomb, except much fancier, with more ornamentation on it and sometimes even the representation of a human body resting on top of it.

HIP TOMB: Hip tombs are easy to identify because the top of this sarcophagus looks like a hip-roofed house. (A hip roof islants inwards at all four sides.) Hip tombs can even just consist of the roof-like structure alone, with no sides to support it.

Hip tombs resemble hip style roofs.

PEDESTAL TOMB: A sarcophagus held up by pedestals, it's simply called a pedestal tomb. These range from simple poles to ornate columns.

Sarcophagus style tomb: has animal paws at the base

SARCOPHAGUS TOMB: I think a better name for these would be "bathtub tomb" because the defining characteristic of this type of this sarcophagus is that it stands on paw-like structures, much like a clawfoot bathtub.

BARREL TOMB: If a tomb has a rounded top, it is called a "barrel tomb." In the USA, these can even be made of brick, although they are usually made of cement.

BALE TOMB: Bale tombs are barrel tombs that include a squiggly design on top. It's not quite clear where this design gets its name. Some say that the "bale" on top is supposed to looked like a wrinkled woolen shroud, and refers back to the woolen shroud that bodies were legally required to be buried in during 17th century England. (On a side note, this is where the saying "pulling the wool over someone's eyes" comes from.)

Jefferson Davis had a catafalque on a carriage

CATAFALQUE: When the body or coffin of a US president or other important government officials on public display, the structure it rests upon is called a catafalque.
The catafalque used to display Abraham Lincoln's body in 1865 and transport him back to Illinois after his assassination was most recently used in 2016 for Supreme Court Judge, Antonin Scalia when he lay in state.
Another famous American catafalque is the one now on

display in Biloxi, Mississippi at Beauvoir, the home of Jefferson Davis. In 1889, Davis was buried in New Orleans. Four years later, he was exhumed and transported to Richmond, Virginia since it had been the capital of the confederacy, and he, their elected president. As Davis' body journeyed to Virginia, the public came out in droves to meet his funeral train, and see his casket on this catafalque.

TABLE TOMB: If they weren't made of stone, these structures wouldn't be all that out-of-place in your dining room. Table tombs are easy to spot because, as the name suggests, they look like great big tables.

Table tombs date back to ancient Greece. In those days, a funeral wasn't the only time your family would meet at your grave as a group. Families would meet at gravesite for family celebrations throughout the year.

After a death in the family, the first thing to be erected was most often a table tomb, because this gave people a convenient place to put the food and wine for their celebration.

An exedra is a stone cemetery bench

EXEDRA: After erecting a table stone to place food and wine on during gravesite festivities, ancient Greeks often built a type of stone bench called an exedra. Now the family had a place to sit during their gravesite festivities.

Exedrae may be straight or curved. These benches are for public use, so you can find them in gymnasiums and public squares, as well as burial grounds. If you've ever seen a painting of a Greek philosopher sitting while surrounded by his students, the artist most likely painted him sitting on an exedra.

Ancient Greeks were not allowed to bury their dead within city limits, so the roadways leading into town were lined with burial sites. Rich families would do their best to erect the fanciest, most eye-catching tombs they could afford. Much like billboards line modern highways on the way into town, ancient Greeks used funeral monuments to advertise the most powerful local families.

Exedra-style benches were fashionable graveyard monuments in the Victorian era through the 1920's in America, and are often found on wealthier people's graves. Even when it's not an exedra, you will notice that benches are more common in burial grounds than single chairs.

Ledger stones are large, flat and rectangular

LEDGER STONES: Ledger stones are rectangular burial slabs that lay flat on the ground above a coffin. In this case, the word "ledger" comes from the German word *legen*, meaning "to lie."

WOLF STONES: Wolf stones are a particularly American type of ledger stone. In New England during the 1600's, wolves often raided fresh graves and scattered the remains. It was such a problem that in 1660, Connecticut offered a bounty of 20 shillings (a hefty sum in those days) for each dead wolf.

The term "wolf stone" is not just a colorful turn of phrase, but a very literal description of this ledger stone's function! Few wolf stones remain, at least in New England's graveyards, because once the wolves were eradicated, settlers used these monuments for capstones on stone walls. Times were tough and they could not afford to be too sentimental.

BODY STONE: Like a ledger stone, a body stone lays flat on the ground above a coffin. The only difference is that instead of being rectangular, it is shaped like the outline of a human body, and looks rather like a mummy. These are not common in the United States.

Coffin stones are shaped like a six-sided coffin

COFFIN STONE: Like ledger stones and body stones, coffin stones also lay flat on the ground. The only difference is that coffin stones, as you may have guessed, are shaped like a six-sided coffin.

COFFIN VS CASKET

This is probably a good time to point out that while the words "coffin" and "casket" are often used interchangeably, in America they are slightly different things. The word "coffin" comes from the ancient Greek word *kophinos*, meaning "basket." Coffins are narrow at the head and foot, but wider at the shoulders, in what is sometimes referred to as an anthropoid shape. Caskets, on the other hand, are rectangular shaped. So, while they both function as containers for the deceased, a coffin is simply a different style than a casket.

Until the late 1800's, coffins and caskets were not a mass-produced item in America. It was the tremendous loss of life during the Civil War that gave birth to the coffin industry. The Civil War also made embalming the norm, because of the need to transport bodies back to their home states for burial.

In cities, you might find coffins for sale at the local furniture store. Furniture stores often branched out and became morgues and funeral homes. And if an unlucky soul perished while visiting another town and did not have any identification, they were likely to be embalmed and placed in the display window of the store in the hopes that a passerby might recognize them. This may seem shocking to us now, but I have come across many instances where that happened.

It was not unheard of for people to build their *own* casket years in advance, then stand it upright in a corner of their home and use it as shelves until it was needed otherwise. While this might strike our modern sensibilities as morbid, back then it was simply considered practical.

After the Civil War, and with the rise of garden cemeteries and the symbology embraced during the Victorian Era, funeral directors introduced an alternative to the coffin. Called a casket, this style of container is rectangular shaped. It's usually padded and has pillows and even blankets inside. It's meant to tie in with the idea of the deceased being at eternal rest. At that time, the word "casket" meant a box to hold trinkets and jewelry.

Not everyone was impressed by the idea of caskets and the euphemism they promoted. In his 1863 book of essays entitled *Our Old Home,* Nathaniel Hawthorne complained about this newfangled container for the deceased, writing, "Caskets! - a vile modern phrase which compels a person of sense and good taste to shrink more disgustfully than ever before from the idea of being buried at all."

MORTSAFES:

Mortsafes are exceedingly rare in America, but they have a fascinating history. These days, people often make arrangements to donate their body to science after they die. We accept the fact that medical students need cadavers to learn about human anatomy. But this was not always the case.

Until the mid-1800's, the only way for medical students to get practice cadavers was to steal them from graveyards! As a result, professional body snatchers, called Resurrectionists, sack 'em up men, or simply grave robbers, sold stolen cadavers to anatomists, hospitals and universities. Sometimes, the medical students themselves were the grave robbers!

As you can imagine, no one wanted the body of a beloved family members snatched from its grave, and not simply because it was disrespectful. At this time, many people truly believed they needed their physical body intact for the second coming of Christ. Amputees might even bury their limbs so they could retrieve them on Judgment Day. The idea of donating your body to science was frightening because it might possibly rob you of a chance for eternal life.

The middle box tomb contains an amputated arm, not body!

People found the idea so distasteful that from 1785 to 1855, there were at least 17 riots by the American public in response to medical schools' use of cadavers.

One horrific example dates to 1852, when an Ohio family discovered their daughter missing from her grave. Later, the father heard rumors that the body parts of a young woman had been found in a medical school's cesspool in Cleveland. As the father and his friends confronted the medical students there, an angry mob gathered outside. When the father discovered his daughter's hand on the premise, a riot broke out and the building was set on fire.

It's easy to understand how Mary Shelley's 1818 book, *Frankenstein,* about grave robbery and sinister science gone awry fed right into some very real fears.

One way to combat grave robbers was to erect heavy metal cages over fresh graves. Called "mortsafes," these devices first appeared in Scotland in the early 1800's. Why Scotland? Edinburgh featured several prominent medical universities, so Resurrectionists were very active in the surrounding area.

Mortsafes were often rented by the family from either the church or the cemetery for a few weeks, after which the cage would be removed and used by another grieving family. Since mortsafes were not meant to be permanent structures, very few remain standing today, even in Scotland.

From my research, it does not appear that mortsafes were used as much in the USA. Instead, those who could afford it might simply hire night watchmen for the first few weeks after burial, or even enlist the help of their friends and family to hold vigil. Others used elaborate burglar-proof coffins. Some caskets were even wired to blow up if they were opened. Another tactic for preventing grave robbery involved adding several layers of straw to the dirt during burial.

One more defense against Resurrectionists was to leave the body in what's called a "receiving vault" for several weeks. Medical students required fresh cadavers, so if you waited long enough, you would keep the body of your loved one safe. When you visit a historic graveyard, pay attention to old storage buildings. Older buildings that are now used to house lawn mowers and other tools may actually have once been receiving vaults.

Receiving vaults had other uses than protecting against grave robbers. In winter months, they provided a place to store corpses until the ground thawed enough for burial.

The only two remaining examples of mortsafes I could find in the USA are in Catawissa, Pennsylvania. Known locally as "hooded graves," these burial sites feature elaborate metal cages on top of them. Once clue that these are mortsafes is that the cages are locked. This suggests they are meant to keep humans out, not simply animals.

As mentioned earlier, mortsafes were not mean to be permanent structures, so it's odd that the graves in Catawissa still have them. In fact, in this particular case, some speculate that the metal cages were placed there to keep the dead inside the graves rather than to keep the living out!

Grave houses in Istre, LA are large and sturdy

GRAVE HOUSES, GRAVE SHELTERS & SPIRIT HOUSES:

As the names suggest, these gravesite structures look like miniature houses. They are seen primarily through the

South and while usually wooden, they are sometimes made of stone or brick.

Although their purpose is debatable, in the Upland South (Virginia, North Carolina, Tennessee, Arkansas, as well as portions of Kentucky, Missouri, West Virginia, Maryland) these structures are primarily called Grave Houses. They are most often seen in hilltop cemeteries. Rural communities often created hilltop burial grounds not for any sentimental reasons, such as giving the deceased a better view, but simply because it kept the burial grounds separate from the fields they tended below.

Throughout Louisiana and other parts of the South, Catholics tend to call these little buildings Grave Houses, while Protestants tend to call them Grave Shelters. When erected by Native Americans, however, they are usually referred to as Spirit Houses.

Most grave shelters are less sturdy, like this one in Texas

Whatever they are are called locally, these little houses are a rare site. Depending on the area and prevailing religious customs, they will either be empty or contain photos, candles, rosaries, flowers, and religious icons.

So what is the purpose for building miniature houses at a gravesite? Stories passed down about these structures often say something like, "He didn't want rain to fall on his grave." My research, so far, has not come up anything conclusive.

On a practical level, Grave Houses may keep livestock from grazing or trampling a grave. But why would people only do this on a few graves in a cemetery and not all of them if this were the case?

Another theory, and one that seems more likely to me, at least for Christians, is that these miniature houses are a reference to the biblical verse John 14:2, which says, "In my Father's house are many mansions: if it were not so, I would have told you. I go to prepare a place for you."

Bolster style monument

BOLSTER:
Bolster style monuments feature cylindrically shaped stones and are meant to represent pillows.

FLOWER BOXES:
The Victorians often created a little raised rectangular shape outlining the perimeter of the grave. Family members would then plant flowers inside this raised planter area.

Flower Box style graves were planted with flowers

CRADLES:
Flower box style graves for children are often called "cradles."

FOLK STYLE MONUMENTS:
This is a catchall term for handmade monuments, they are more common in impoverished areas and are often inspired by economic necessity. Folk style monuments come in a wide variety of styles and may feature petrified wood, marbles and even PVC pipe.

OBELISKS:
Obelisks are a common sight in historic cemeteries throughout the United States. (See Chapter 11 for examples.)

11 CEMETERY ARCHITECTURE

While cemetery monuments often echo the urban architecture of their time and place, it is here, too, that people often mix and match different styles to suit their most whimsical of whims. And why not? Just as there are no fashion police to ensure that your outfits match, there are no rules saying that you can't mix and match your favorite symbols and architectural styles. After all, a cemetery monument is your last chance to make a good impression.

Like so much of this book, this is a big topic. If you are a student of architecture, it is not my intention to offend you. I realize, for instance, that what I lump together as Classical Revival, could be further broken down into Neoclassical, Greek Revival, Roman Revival and even more precise subsets. For the purposes of this guide, however, I have divided the styles of architecture most commonly found in American cemeteries into 10 very broad categories

Even with these 10 categories, a monument can fall into two or more categories. As mentioned before, people often combine different styles to suit their fancy. A pyramid, for instance, could certainly be considered Ancient Pagan, but Egyptian Revival style structures and symbols are so common in American graveyards that I felt they warranted their own category.

ANCIENT PAGAN:

Ancient Pagan style refers to modern versions of ancient structures found in historic graveyards such as the tumulus, grotto and cairn. I described cairns earlier, but here's a description for the other two.

Tumulus style tomb for Elks Club members

TUMULUS:

The Tumulus is a special kind of burial mound. It starts as a cairn, then dirt is heaped up on it to create a rounded hill. In ancient times, a tumulus was used to bury either a group of soldiers or perhaps to honor one specific great warrior.

When you see a tumulus in modern American cemeteries, they are usually associated with a fraternal organization or military society. The one pictured below is in New Orleans' Greenwood Cemetery.

GROTTO:

A grotto is meant to look like a little cave. The practice of putting religious icons and statuary in the nooks of little caves dates back to the ancient Greeks, but today they are most commonly found in Catholic cemeteries.

A grotto is meant to look like a cave.

EGYPTIAN REVIVAL:

After invading Egypt in the late 1790's, Napoleon returned with such exotic plunder that all things Egyptian were fashionable in Europe and America. And so it has been with every subsequent major excavation of Egyptian tombs. We've all probably seen enough movies and TV shows about Cleopatra and cursed mummies to recognize a pyramid or an ankh. Even as I write this in 2017, a major motion picture entitled "The Mummy" has just been released.

America's fascination with ancient Egypt makes this style of architecture easy to spot. Here are a few hallmarks of Egyptian Revival architecture to watch for when you visit a historic cemetery:

ANKH:

The ankh gets its name from an ancient Egyptian hieroglyph meaning "breath of life." As a symbol, the ankh represented eternal life to ancient Egyptians. Their gods are often shown touching the lips of the departed with an ankh to reawaken their souls to the afterlife.

Coptic Christians later adopted the ankh as a symbol of Christ's resurrection. Due to its shape, they called it the *crux ansata*, which is Latin for "cross with a handle." Even today, when an ankh appears on a Christian's grave, it most likely signifies eternal life and the resurrection.

Lotus leaf topped column & pyramid with sphinx

EGYPTIAN COLUMNS:

Egyptian columns are often topped with a lotus leaf design. This is a quick way to make sure it is an Egyptian Revival column rather than a Classical style. (I'll describe those later in this chapter.) Also, since Egyptians had not mastered creating arches, their entryways have squared-off tops rather than archways.

LOTUS FLOWER:

The lotus flower, also known as the water lily, is an important ancient Egyptian symbol. Since the lotus blooms during the day but closes at night, it is a symbol of rebirth When adopted by Christians, it refers to the resurrection and afterlife.

OBELISKS:

Obelisks are a common sight in historic cemeteries throughout the United States. The pointed tip, which was often guilded or painted gold, represents a ray of sunlight reaching down from the heavens and connecting with the mortals on earth. How did this ancient Egyptian form work its way into Christian symbology?

Although they've existed for thousands of years, obelisks gained popularity after Napoleon invaded Egypt in the late 1700's. As the form began to appear in Classical architecture throughout America (the Washington Monument is an impressive example), it made its way into graveyards, as well.

To our nation's founding fathers, the obelisk represented a connection between heaven and earth, as well as power, strength, and fatherhood.

As a Christian symbol, the obelisk also represents how a person becomes more focused on spiritual goals as they mature. As the wide base of the obelisk narrows, it symbolizes how a soul reunites with God at death by becoming one with him.

In historic cemeteries, an obelisk is often at the center of a family plot, where it represents the family's connection to the heavenly father.

OBELISK VARIATIONS: Victorians riffed on the obelisk form and created several variations. Here are a couple you might see in historic graveyards:

TRUNCATED OBELISK:
A truncated obelisk is an obelisk form that does not come to a sharp point, and is either flat, or topped with another item, such as an urn, orb or cube.

VAULTED OBELISK:
This is an obelisk that, instead of coming to one single point, has points on all four sides, rather like the vaulted ceiling of a church.

Regular obelisk, Truncated, Truncated with orb, Vaulted

PYRAMIDS:
A pyramid is the most obvious Egyptian symbol and makes an impressive monument. The grave for the famous Native American chief, Geronimo, for instance, is in the shape of a pyramid. More recently, the actor, Nicolas Cage, commissioned a pyramid-shaped mausoleum for himself.

The word "pyramid" comes from the ancient Greek word, *pyramis* meaning "wheaten cake" because its shape reminded them of pastries. The ancient Egyptian word for pyramid (*mer*) meaning "place of ascension" provides a better clue regarding the original purpose for these grand burial chambers. Since they were used for burial, ancient pyramids were always built on the west side of the Nile, where the sun sets each night.

Just like an obelisk, pyramids are wide at the bottom and come to a point at the top. Once again, this stems from Egyptian sun worship. Like an obelisk, the pointed end of a pyramid represents a beam of sunlight coming down from the heavens to connect to earth.

In America, Christians sometimes joke that the sharp point of a pyramid keeps Satan from sitting on a grave. As a modern symbol, the pyramid stands for eternity, eternal life and/or spiritual enlightenment.

SCARAB: Considering that they have featured in jewelry and artwork since ancient Egyptian times, scarabs must be the most glamorous dung beetles in the world. As a symbol adopted by Christians, the scarab symbolizes spiritual transcendence and the renewal of life.

SPHINX:

Egyptian Revival style monuments may include a mythical creature called a sphinx. You will often find a pair of them guarding the entrance to mausoleums.

A sphinx has the head of a human and the body of a lion. True Egyptian sphinxes are always male. If you see a female sphinx, it is a Greek-influenced image.

VULTURE WINGS:

To ancient Egyptians, vultures were a symbol for motherhood. This is because, unlike many smaller birds,

Sphinx in Lake Lawn Metairie Cemetery, New Orleans, LA

vultures require a lot of care and nurture before they leave the nest.

Vulture wings often feature a circle shape in the middle. This represents the sun god Ra, from whom all life springs. Look closely and you may also see a pair of snakes, one on either side of this sun disc. These are cobras, highly venomous snakes meant to symbolize death.

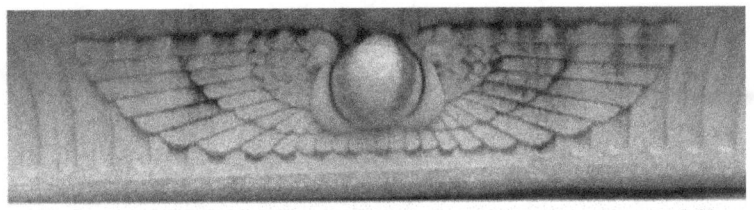

Vulture wings: cobras flank the sun disc in the middle

CLASSICAL (GRECO ROMAN) REVIVAL:

Classical Revival style architecture is seen throughout America, and not just in historic cemeteries. Many public buildings feature Classical Revival style design. Our forefathers were attracted to ancient Greek and Roman architecture not only because they liked how it looked, but also because they liked what it represented.

Ancient Greeks were the first civilization to create cities meant to be owned, used, and ruled by the people, rather than by royalty. They called this new system for people to live together a *polis*.

In kingdoms, all the land and main structures are owned by the king. A *polis*, however, features spaces and buildings that are open to the public and free to use.

Today, it's easy to take public libraries, parks, and other public spaces for granted, but America's founding fathers certainly did not.

Incorporating Greek and Roman style architecture into their public buildings was a symbolic way to express how they were creating a government of the people, by the people, and for they people.

Classical Revival elements are easy to identify in buildings and monuments. Look for Greco-Roman style columns, rounded arches, and a boxy look over all.

Columns that are not Egyptian style are a prominent feature in most Classical Revival style architecture. Here are some quick tips for identifying different styles of columns:

DORIC COLUMNS: These columns are the most plain-looking of column types and have squared-looking capitals, or tops.

IONIAN COLUMNS: Ionian columns feature a rounded scroll shape. They are often described as having feminine characteristics due to their spirals and more slender design.

CORINTHIAN: Corinthian columns are topped with an acanthus leaf design. Even if you've never seen an acanthus plant in real life, its leaves are such a common design motif that it probably looks familiar. To ancient Greeks, acanthus leaves represented hardiness against the trials of life and immortality. To Christians, the thorny leaves of the acanthus signify sin and punishment.

Some designers can't resist adding other plants, such as ferns and ivy to Corinthian columns. You may even spot the occasional flower, bird, or chipmunk in the foliage.

COMPOSITE: These are the fanciest looking type of columns because they combine design elements from two or more column styles, for instance, a column featuring Corinthian style foliage with rounded Ionic capitals added to the mix.

Classical columns from left to right:
Ionian, Doric, Corinthian & Composite

BYZANTINE REVIVAL:
While this style of architecture is not common in American cemeteries, you may still spot touches of it here and there. Look for mosaics, onion domes, and horseshoe-shaped arches.

GOTHIC REVIVAL:
Like Egyptian Revival, this is another form of architectural style that most of us are familiar with thanks

to Hollywood, especially in movies about haunted houses,

A quick way to spot Gothic Revival is to look for pointed arches rather than the rounded Roman style arches you see with Classical Revival. The pointed shape is meant to look like hands clasped in prayer, and is a common feature in church windows. Other clues include tall spires, and design elements called trefoils, quatrefoils and cinquefoils.

TRIQUETRA: A triquetra consists of three interlocking circles or triangles. It's also called a trefoil. In either case, this design often appears on Celtic crosses to represent the Holy Trinity.

QUATREFOIL: This form is often part of an overall Gothic style of architecture. The four lobes of a quatrefoil stand for the four Evangelists (Matthew, Mark, Luke, John.)

CINQUEFOIL: Not as common as the others, a cinquefoil consists of five interlocking circles. As a symbols, it stands for the bond between mother and daughter.

Mausoleums: Classical Revival (left), Rustic Style (right)

In fact, unlike all the other styles of architecture described so far, this one was not adopted from by Christians from other cultures. Gothic style architecture was actually created by Christians during the Middle Ages.

The word itself comes from the Italians who made fun of the first gothic cathedrals built by the French. They claimed the buildings were so ugly they must have been built by goths, and the name stuck.

RUSTIC STYLE:

In late 1800's and early 1900's, masons often gave large stones in public buildings a rough hewn look, called rustic style or rustication.

Like other popular architectural styles, the rustic style is seen in historic graveyards of that time. While it can simply be a design preference, such as when the sides of a headstone are rustic, there can also be a symbolic meaning.

When you see a monument that is half-polished and half-rusticated, it represents the transition from life into death. It also expresses the idea that while we may accomplish many things during our time on earth, we have even more to learn and do in the afterlife. Our soul's evolution continues after death.

Classical Revival (left & mid), Byzantine Revival (right)

ART NOUVEAU:

Art Nouveau style architecture was popular from 1890 through the 1920's in the USA. This style is often seen on mausoleums from that time period and features curved lines, and asymmetric designs that are flowing, wispy, and delicate. Art Nouveau ornamentation is meant to echo the forms we see in nature, or what we might now call fractals.

ART DECO:

In 1925, a Parisian design expo launched Art Deco, a new style of architecture with a smooth, sleek look. Everything from cars, fabric designs, and fonts were affected by this style through the 1930's.

Art Deco mausoleums are boxy yet streamlined, with clusters of lines and geometric patterns. To me, Art Deco design elements are often reminiscent of the grills on vintage vehicles. When Art Deco structures include human figures, they are more stylized, with a geometric look to them, rather than having the realistic features of Classical Revival statues.

FOLK ARCHITECTURE:

Folk Architecture covers a lot of ground, literally and figuratively. This is simply a catchall term to describe everything from grave houses and handmade markers, to unique monuments handmade by the friends and family of the deceased.

Obviously, not everyone can afford a fancy gravestone, so Folk Architecture is most often seen in impoverished areas. It may also simply be a personal choice.

MODERN ARCHITECTURE

This is another catchall term used to describe

monuments created from the mid-20th century through the present.

Modern Style monuments in Palestine, TX

12 HANDS, HEARTS & BODY PARTS

While human figures in a historic graveyard often represent a specific angel, saint or other being, that's not always the case. Sometimes the parts of the human body appear on their own to convey symbolic messages to the viewer.

SKULL AND CROSSBONES IN CONTEXT

As mentioned before, early epitaphs could be quite stern. It's the same with tombstone imagery from the 16th and 17th century in America.

Skulls, or a skull and crossbones, are frequently seen on these early headstones. Back then, skulls and other mortality symbols served to remind the living of the fleetness of life, and that they had better behave while they were alive.

In the 21st century, however, skulls may have a different connotation. I once toured London's Highgate Cemetery with a group of people that included members of a motorcycle club. As the tour guide pointed out various mortality symbols, I noticed that many of the bikers in our tour had skulls on their clothing.

Today, skulls aren't simply a mortality symbol; they also convey a sense of machismo and the idea that someone is a daredevil. America's Puritans certainly weren't trying to be macho or impress us by how tough they were. They lived in a time and place when simply trying to make it from one day to the next was challenging enough. Just like other symbols, the meaning of skulls depends upon its context in time, place, and religious belief.

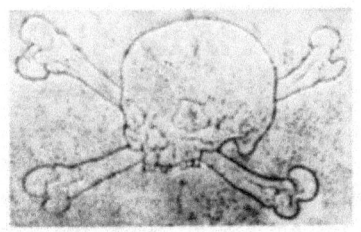 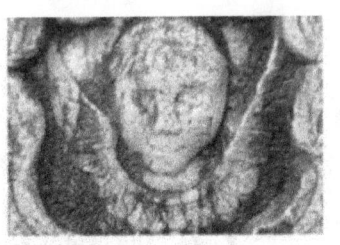

Skull & crossbones evolved into Soul effigies

FROM SOUL EFFIGIES TO CHERUBS

As the Puritans' grim outlook on life began to ease its grip on America's psyche, the imagery used on tombstones began changing, too. By the 1690's, skulls were gradually displaced by a human face with wings.

Sometimes called "soul effigies," these winged faces were not meant to be an accurate representation of any particular person. Instead, they symbolize the soul's flight to Heaven.

By the Victorian Era, soul effigies were eclipsed by children's faces with wings, as well as sweet-faced cherubs and winged toddlers.

In addition to the human face, the rest of this chapter describes the possible symbolism behind hands, hearts, and other body parts in historic graveyards of America.

Winged faces & a Victorian Era cherub

SKULLS & FACES

SKULL AND/OR SKULL AND CROSSBONES: The earliest human forms to appear on American headstones are the skulls and crossbones on Puritans' grave markers. These bones are meant as a reminder of the inevitability of death.

SKULL WITH CROWN: A skull either wearing or next to a crown represents the soul's triumph over death.

SKULL WITH CROWN OF THORNS: A skull with a crown of thorns represents the torment of the spirit.

SKULL WITH WINGS: Stands for the soul's flight to Heaven.

WINGED FACES: Also stands for the soul's flight to Heaven.

CHERUBS: By the Victorian Era, chubby babies and even toddlers with wings were used to represent innocence.

HAIR: The engravings and statues of women in graveyards quite often show them with long, flowing hair, hair that hangs loose rather than being clipped or tied back. Long hair symbolizes acts of penance and refers to a Biblical verse John 7:37-38 in which a female sinner bathes the feet of Jesus with her tears before wiping them dry with her hair.

Arms pleading for mercy

ARMS REACHING OUT: This is a plea for God's mercy and forgiveness.

ARMS IN FRONT OF A CROSS: This emblem may refer to the Franciscan Order of monks. Look to see if there are any wounds shown on either of the hands. If the arm is bare and has a wound in the palm, it represents Christ on the cross. If the other arm shown wears a robe, but also has a wound on the palm, it stands for the stigmata St. Francis of Assisi, because he had a stigmata.

HANDS

HANDS, IN GENERAL: Just as we make gestures when we speak to emphasize a point or clarify emotions, when hands are shown in cemetery art, they often have a message to convey. Here are some possibilities to consider when decoding the symbology of hands in historic graveyards:

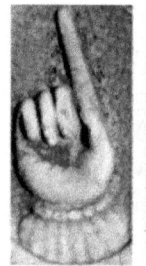  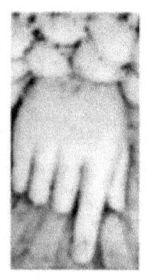  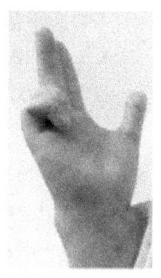

Hands from left to right: Pointing up, Pointing to a crown, Pointing down, Heart in palm, Manus Dei blessing

HAND OF GOD: When you see a hand reaching out of the clouds, you are looking at the hand of God, reaching down from Heaven.

HANDS BLESSING: A hand held upright with the first two fingers together, and the other two held down by the thumb, is the *Manus Dei*, Latin for "hand of God."

The Manus Dei is often used in a cemetery to mark the grave of a member of the clergy.

Depending on the deceased's religion, you may also see a Greek form of the Manus Dei, in which the first two fingers, along with the pinky, are held up while the ring finger is held down by the thumb. In this case, the three upright fingers stand for the Holy Trinity.

When the deceased is not a member of the church, the

Manus Dei is simply a way to bestow a blessing upon the living relatives who remain on earth.

HAND WITH A HEART IN THE PALM: A hand with a heart in the palm, symbolizes charity and generosity. It is often associated with the International Order of Oddfellows.

HANDS OF COHEN: If you are a Star Trek fan, you may be surprised to see a pair of hands, seemingly giving Commander Spock's famous "Live long and prosper" gesture, engraved on a headstone.

As it happens, Leonard Nimoy, who played Spock in the famous TV show, was Jewish. As a child, he saw some members of his church making this sign. Later, he proposed it for the famous science fiction show.

When you see "Spock hands" on a tomb, you are actually looking at "Cohen hands," also called, the "Hands of Kohanim." This hand gesture signifies that the deceased is Jewish person who descended from the priestly Tribe of Cohen.

Incidentally, Cohen descendants are forbidden from attending funerals, except in the case of their relatives and closest friends.

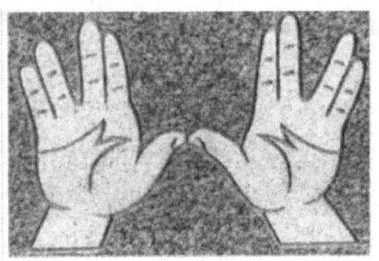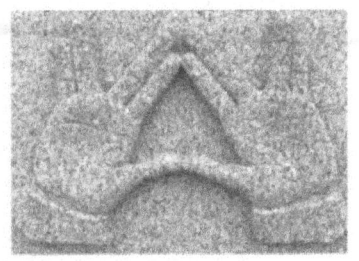

Two examples of Cohen hands

HAND HOLDING A CROSS: When you see a hand holding a cross, it is a reminder of Christ's resurrection and the eternal life of the soul.

HAND HOLDING AN ORB: When you see a figure holding an orb, it stands for Christ's dominion over the world. When the orb features a Latin cross sticking out of it, it is called a *globus cruciger*, or "cross-bearing orb.

HAND POINTING UP: When you see a hand pointing up, it means that the deceased has gone to Heaven.

HAND POINTING DOWN: Since a hand pointing up means a person is on their way to Heaven, you might be a little worried when you see a hand pointing straight down. While this does not imply that the person is going the Hell, it often indicated that the person died abruptly and unexpectedly, such as a woman in childbirth, or as the result of some kind of accident.

HANDS PRAYING: When you see hands clasped in prayer, it is expressing the deceased's pious devotion and is a plea to God for eternal life.

Palms held out as a blessing. Hand on neck for sacrifice

HAND RESTING ON CHEST: When a human figure is shown with a hand resting on his or her chest, it is symbolic shorthand for divine wisdom. If it's a female figure and she appears to be holding onto her garment at chest level, you may be looking at the Virtue of Charity.

HAND RESTING ON NECK: When a hand is seen resting on the neck of a figure, it is symbolic shorthand for sacrifice, and may indicate a martyred saint.

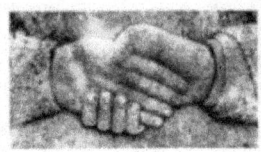  

Handshake: Fraternal (left), Limp fingers (mid), Marital (right)

HANDSHAKES: When you see a handshake on a grave marker, try to figure out the gender of those depicted. If it's two males, then the handshake likely stands for fraternal brotherhood.

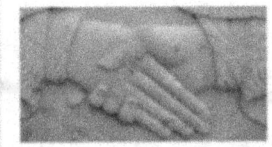 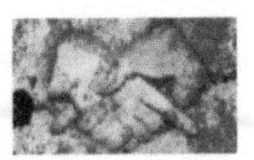 

Masonic (left), Double Masonic (mid), Masonic emblem (rt.)

Handshakes can simply stand for God or other loved ones welcoming the new soul to Heaven. Handshakes often depict the limp fingers of the deceased firmly gripped by a relative, angelic being, or perhaps even God, himself.

If the gender shown is obviously male and female, it's

most likely a marital handshake, meant to show that the deceased was married

When one finger is extended, it means that the deceased was a member of the Freemasons. If a husband and wife are buried together and both were Masons, then you will see a Double Masonic handshake. A Mason I spoke explained this is meant to resemble the compass and square Masonic emblem. As you can see below, it really does.

HEARTS

HEART: The heart is an easily recognized and commonly used symbol for love and devotion. Like hands, however, there are some variations that mean specific things:

Flaming heart with thorns & rays of God's glory

Ivy covered heart in Galveston City Cemetery

BLEEDING HEART: When you see a heart that appears to be bleeding, it symbolizes the suffering and torment of Christ.

FLAMING HEART: A flaming heart is symbolic of a human soul burning with religious zeal.

HEART HELD IN HANDS: When you see a heart gently cradled in a pair of hands it stands for love and piety.

HEART COVERED WITH IVY: Love combined with enduring friendship and faithfulness.

TWO HEARTS JOINED TOGETHER: This is a common symbol for two hearts joined together by marriage.

HEART WITH THORNS: Catholic graves sometimes feature a heart surrounded by thorns and topped with a cross. Called the "Sacred Heart," this image is meant to remind the devout how Jesus died for their sins.

HEART PIERCED BY A SWORD: This is another Catholic symbol which is known as the Immaculate Heart of Mary. As a symbol, it stands for devotion, sorrow and repentance.

13 SAINTS, ANGELS & OTHER BEINGS

Human figures featured in the statuary of historic graveyards often represent specific saints, angels, and other beings.

As you begin looking more closely at the statues n historic graveyards, you may notice that sometimes the Virtues and even some saints, are shown with wings. Shouldn't angels be the only winged beings?

The word "angel" comes from *angelos,* the Greek word for messenger. The Hebrew word for "angel" is malak, also meaning "messenger." According to ancient tradition, a genuinely angelic being has never lived on earth as a human, even though it may take human form to communicate with us.

While it's true that angels are winged beings, they are not the only human figures you will see with wings. Why, then are some figures other than angels often shown with wings? When wings are added to a human figure, it is meant as symbolic shorthand. The Latin word for "saint" is *sancta*, meaning "holy." The moment any one of us reaches heaven, we, too, become holy. So adding wings to a human figure is a symbolic way of saying that the deceased is now in heaven. For the same reason, a statue of a winged child at a grave is most likely a way to express that this little one is now in Heaven.

As you search for saints, angels and virtues in the graveyard, don't get too hung up on whether or not they have wings.

Recording Angels always have a book & a pen with them.

WHO'S WHO?

Here's a guide to some of the most common saints, angels and other beings you will see depicted in historic American burial grounds.

ANGEL HOLDING A BOOK: An angel holding a book, and even, perhaps, holding a feather pen and writing is a celestial scribe known simply as a "Recording Angel."

FLYING ANGEL: An angel in flight, sometimes even shown with a mortal in tow, symbolizes the deceased person's ascent to Heaven.

WEEPING ANGEL: These mourning angels symbolize grief and sorrow.

PRAYING ANGEL: A praying angel symbolizes religious faith.

Angels hold flowers to symbolize life's fleeting quality.

ANGEL HOLDING A WREATH: Stands for Memory and eternity, letting us know that this person's life will not be forgotten.

SAINT HOLDING A PALM FROND: When a saint holds a palm frond in one hand it is a symbol of their martydom.

ST. ANTHONY OF EGYPT: St. Anthony of Egypt is the patron saint of gravediggers. Many taphophiles believe this makes him the patron saint of those of us who enjoy exploring historic graveyards, as well.

The reason St. Anthony of Egypt is considered the patron saint of undertakers, gravediggers and cemetery workers is because he sold everything he owned and lived in a tomb at the start of his life's work. Somewhere along the line he healed a sick pig, and the two became lifelong friends.

For this reason, St. Anthony of Egypt is often shown

with his porcine companion seated nearby. There's even an ancient Catholic tradition linked to the feast day for St. Anthony of Egypt which involved bringing your farm animals to the church for a blessing. This tradition still continues in some communities.

Left: St. Joseph   Right: St. Anthony of Padua

ST ANTHONY OF PADUA: This is a different St. Anthony and the one you are much more likely to see depicted in a historic graveyard. He is most often shown holding baby Jesus, as well as a book, because Christ appeared to him in the form of a child while he was reading the Bible.

St. Anthony of Padua is also frequently seen holding a an Easter lily to symbolize his purity and innocence. Lilies are so closely associated with St. Antony of Padua that when Catholics make a special anointing oil from pressed lily flowers, it is called "St. Anthony's Oil."

The Virgin Mary's husband, Joseph, may also be seen

holding baby Jesus and a lily. St. Anthony, however, will have a monk's robe and haircut, and will also be holding a book.

Jesus Christ may be depicted as an adult or a child.

ST CECILIA: St. Cecilia became the patron saint of music and musicians because she heard music in her heart on her wedding day. She is often shown holding a harp or with organ pipes near her.

CHARON: Charon is the angel of death often shown towing a boat with the body of the deceased to the other side. (By the way, it's acceptable to pronounce the "ch" in Charon as either a "sh," "ch," or hard "k" sound.) The body of water Charon is crossing is the mythical River Styx, which, according to an ancient Greek myth, separates the living from the dead.

FATHER TIME: Although they are both often depicted holding an hourglass, sickle, or staff, Father Time is an old gentleman with a long flowing beard. He may, at times, be shown with wings, but they are not mandatory. The Grim Reaper, on the other hand, is an emaciated figure, or even a skeleton.

The Virgin Mary may be depicted several different ways.

FOUR EVANGELISTS: Matthew, Mark, Luke and John, the men who wrote the first four books of the Bible, are known collectively as the Four Evangelists.

Each one of the four is associated with unique symbols in literature and art, and this carries over to how they are depicted in cemeteries.

All four sometimes appear at the base of a fancy monument, with a different evangelist in each corner to represent the four corners of the earth. When the evangelists are shown together like this, it is called a Tetraform.

Matthew, Mark, Luke and John are also linked to four signs of the zodiac: Aquarius, Leo, Scorpio, and Taurus, respectively. Today's church has little to do with astrology, but there was no taboo against it in early Christianity, mostly because there was little distinction made between astrology and astronomy.

After all, in the days before the widespread use of paper calendars, the signs of the zodiac helped mark the passing of each year, and several Christian festivals are related to the sky. Easter is celebrated on the first Sunday after the first full moon that occurs on or after the Spring Equinox. So unlike Christmas, which is celebrated annually on December 25, there is no fixed date for Easter.

ST. MATTHEW (winged angel face, Aquarius): In Christian religious art, Saint Matthew is often depicted as an angel. This may be done with either a face or an entire man with wings. So it is possible when you see a male angel that it is meant to be Saint Matthew.

ST. MARK (winged lion, Leo): Saint Mark is often depicted as a lion with wings because his writings emphasized the idea of Christ as king, and lions have long been associated with royalty. Since he was Saint Peter's secretary, he may also appear as a man holding a pen.

ST. LUKE (winged ox, Taurus): Saint Luke appears as an ox with wings, although you could easily mistake this for a flying cow. The ox was chosen to represent St. Luke because it is a sacrificial animal and Luke's writings emphasize the sacrifices that Jesus made for mankind. He may also be shown holding a paintbrush, since he was an artist as well as a doctor.

ST. JOHN (winged eagle, Scorpio): A winged eagle was chosen as symbolic shorthand for Saint John because his gospel focuses on Christ's highest achievements, and just like an eagle, Jesus Christ rose to great heights. John may also be shown holding a chalice with a snake inside it as a reference to the Roman's attempts to poison him.

Angel Gabriel is easy to find: Just look for his horn.

TETRAFORM: Sometimes, the four evangelists are combined into one shape. When you see this, it is called a Tetraform.

ST FRANCIS OF ASSISI: St. Francis is the patron saint of animals and ecology. He was known for the love he showed to all God's creatures, and would even give sermons to animals.

In the cemetery, St. Francis of Assisi is often depicted as a robed monk. He is usually shown with an animal or two. Often a deer leans affectionately against his legs while a dove perches on his arm or shoulder. Unsurprisingly, St. Francis is a common figure in pet cemeteries.

St. Michael wears armor, wields a sword & slays dragons.

GABRIEL: The angel Gabriel is easy to spot, just look for a horn at his side. Gabriel is the angel who will sound his trumpet on Judgment Day. Some sculptures may even show him about to blow into it, but usually it is tucked against him as he awaits.

GREEN MAN: The Green Man is not a common sight in America, but you may occasionally see his face peering out from the foliage carved on a tomb. In fact, his face will often appear to be made of acanthus leaves. As a symbol, he represents the cycle of life from death to rebirth.

GRIM REAPER: The Grim Reaper is a creepy figure usually represented by either a skeleton or a sickly thin fellow brandishing a large scythe for harvesting souls.

ST LUCIA OF SYRACUSE: St. Lucia is not common, but she is easy to identify. Lucia became a saint after having her eyes gouged out, so you will find her holding a dish with her eyeballs on it. As you might guess, St. Lucia is the patron saint of the blind.

ST MICHAEL: St. Michael is an angelic warrior often depicted defeating Satan, a serpent, or even a dragon. St. Michael is the patron saint of police departments because, like them, he battles with evil. He is often dressed in full armor like a knight.

Since one of St. Michael's duties is to weigh the souls of the dead on Judgment Day, he may also be depicted as a male figure holding a set of scales.

MORONI: Moroni is the angel who appeared to Joseph Smith several times throughout his life and inspired him to found the Church of Jesus Christ of Latter Day Saints, a.k.a. Mormonism.

Like Gabriel, the angel Moroni appears with a horn. Moroni is an important figure to members of the Mormon church, so use context clues to determine whether the horn-bearing angel you are viewing is Gabriel or Moroni.

MOTHER MARY: While she is actually quite easy to recognize, Mother Mary, also known as the Virgin Mary, may be depicted so many different ways in historic cemeteries that it's hard to narrow it down to a brief description.

For instance, Mary might simply appear as a robed woman with her hands clasped in prayer. She often stands with extended hands, palms forward, to bestow a blessing upon the living. She may also have baby Jesus on her lap, or be shown cradling the adult Jesus after the crucifixion.

ST. RAPHAEL: In cemeteries, St. Raphael is usually shown standing beside a little boy who is holding a fish.

Left to right: St Roch, Faith & Remembrance, St Patrick

The child is Tobias, who was nearly devoured when a fish snatched him from the banks of the Tigris River. St. Raphael, also known as "St. Raphael the Healer," not only rescued Tobias, but taught him how to make medicine using the entrails of the very fish that tried to eat him. When Tobias got home, he used this new knowledge to restore his blind father's sight.

SEVEN VIRTUES: The Seven Virtues is a list of traits to which people should aspire. It was originally created by ancient Greek philosophers. Eventually, Christian scholars adopted this list, which they divided into two categories: the Theological Virtues (and calling Faith, Hope and Charity) and the Moral Virtues (Justice, Fortitude, Temperance and Prudence.)

Sometimes these Virtues will be labeled as such on their pedestals, but other times you must use clues to figure out who is who. And just like other human figures, the virtues may or may not have wings.

The Virtue of Faith may appear several different ways.

FAITH: This is a woman leaning on a cross, holding a chalice, or holding a candle or lamp. Sometimes she may even have a flame sprouting from the top of her head!

HOPE: When you see a woman with an anchor beside her, this is Hope. She may even be depicted with a ship on her head, to symbolize the soul's voyage to a new land, but she is more often seen holding a basket of flowers.

CHARITY: In paintings, Charity is often shown nursing a child. In the cemetery, and especially during Victorian times, this symbolism may be toned down quite a bit so that rather than baring her breast, she is merely seen pointing towards her chest, or has a hand lightly tugging at the fabric of her gown.

JUSTICE: More commonly seen in artwork around courtrooms than cemeteries, Justice still makes an appearance every now and then. Look for a female figure

The Virtue of Hope is easy to spot: Just look for her anchor

holding set of scales in her left hand. This symbolizes carefully weighing both sides of an issue. Justice is often blindfolded, to show that she is an impartial judge. Sometimes she also brandishes a sword in her right hand. Its two-sided blade stands for reason and justice.

FORTITUDE: Fortitude is shown as a female warrior, often seen wielding a club or sword and holding a shield. She may be scantily clad.

TEMPERANCE: Temperance often appears on the graves of prohibitionists or other people who advocate clean living. To illustrate this, she will be shown with a water pitcher. Other symbols of Temperance can include a sword left in its sheath to symbolize restraint, or a bridle and bit to symbolize control over one's less than saintly urges.

PRUDENCE: In paintings, Prudence is often shown as a two-headed woman cavorting with a serpent or dragon. As a graveyard statue or engraving, you are more likely to see her as a woman holding a mirror to symbolize the quest for self-knowledge.

Joseph, Mary, Jesus (left), Mary (mid), Virgin of Guadalupe (right)

VIRGIN OF GUADALUPE: The Virgin Mary appeared before an Aztecan man named Juan Diego in 1531. As proof of her divinity, the woman gave him a cloak. When Juan Diego took the cloak to church, roses spilled out to reveal the image of the Virgin of Guadalupe on the fabric. The Virgin of Guadalupe has since become the patron saint of Mexico, so depictions of her are common in areas with a large Hispanic population. Squiggly lines surrounding her body represent rays of sunlight.

14 PLANTS, FLOWERS & TREES

Not every taphophile is a botanist or gardener. Even those who are may find depictions of the plants, flowers and trees in historic graveyards challenging to identify. Unlike real plants, cemetery carvings of plants may be highly stylized or simply inaccurate.

This chapter describes some of the most common plants and trees you may find living in historic burial grounds throughout the USA. It also describes the ones most commonly depicted on grave markers and what they symbolize.

While some plants, such as roses and ferns, are easy to spot, other plants can be tricky to identify on headstones. Engravers use their artistic license to create flowers that aren't completely accurate from a botanical standpoint. They often give plants three leaves, to symbolize the Holy Trinity, for instance. Other variances may be either symbolic or a matter of artistic preference.

Speaking of plants, I sometimes joke that "Evergreen" and "Oakwood" are the "John Smiths" of cemetery names because there are so many burial grounds with those monikers.

THE LANGUAGE OF FLOWERS

Floral symbolism has appeared in artwork for hundreds of years, however during the Victorian Era, this symbolism was developed and codified in more detail than ever before. During the Victorian Era, there was more to the art of flower arranging than simply creating a pretty bouquet. Each blossom had a symbolic meaning. This allowed people to send messages to each other through a bouquet of flowers.

Floriography as the Victorian Language of Flowers is also known, first gained popularity in France before making its way to Britain. Thanks to a series in the *Saturday Evening Post*, the topic gained popularity in America, starting around 1820.

Soon after, a couple of books on the subject including *The Garland of Flora* by Dorothea Dix and *Flora's Dictionary* by Elizabeth Wirt helped popularize this practice in the United States, especially from about 1830 through the 1850's.

While floriography was often used for courtship and flirting, it served a different purpose in the cemetery. As mentioned in Chapter 10, Victorian graves sometimes included a planter box above the above the body. Flowers grown in these plots may have had symbolic significance, as well.

LIVING PLANTS IN BURIAL GROUNDS

In addition to paying attention to plants and flowers engraved on cemetery monuments, pay attention to the living plants, as well. Note any non-native plants you see growing in a cemetery. Often these were planted there not simply because they grow well and look good, but also due to the symbolism they impart.

WHAT STAGE OF LIFE IS THE PLANT IN?

Generally speaking, flowers represent life's fleeting beauty. It's not enough to just think about the species of the engraved plant or flower is, the plant's stage of life may be a symbolic message.

BUD: Indicates a young child.

BROKEN BUD: A broken bud symbolizes the fragility of youth, and is often seen on young children's graves.

DROOPING STEM: A wilted flower or drooping stem is other reference to a young life cut short.

SEVERED STEM: Indicates that a life was cut short.

FULLY BLOSSOMED FLOWER: The person died in the full bloom of their adulthood, perhaps their early twenties.

Left to right: Acacia, Acanthus, Anthemion (palmette)

PLANT SYMBOLISM from A to Z

ACACIA: The acacia plant was used to build the Ark of the Covenant as well as the crown of thorns Christ wore during his crucifixion. On a tombstone, it stands for eternal life and resurrection.

ACANTHUS: The acanthus symbolizes the gardens of Heaven, although it's used so often as a decorative motif that it's easy to overlook. For instance, acanthus leaves are the plant you see on the capitals of Corinthian columns. It's symbolic use dates back to ancient Greece where it grew in the rocky terrain of their cemeteries.

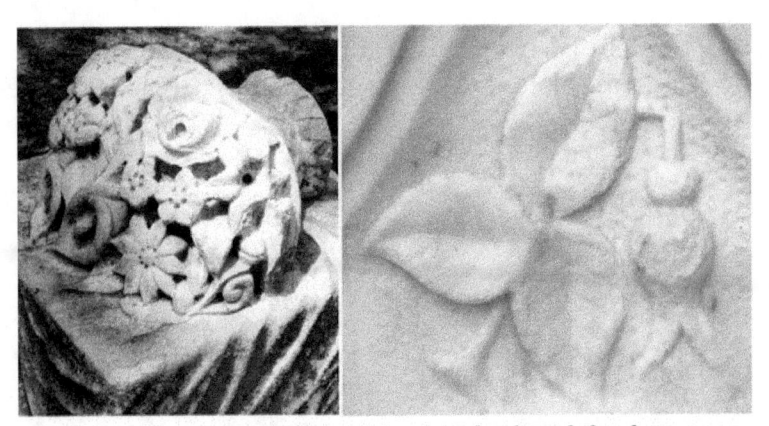

Left to right: Spilled flower basket, bud with broken stem

ACORN: Although oak trees are slow growing, many species live for centuries. Its seed, the acorn, is easily recognizable and symbolizes how greatness may arise from humble beginnings.

ANEMONE: The anemone's bright red blossoms symbolize the blood of Christ. Since the bloom of these flowers is quick to wilt, anemones also represent the brevity of life.

 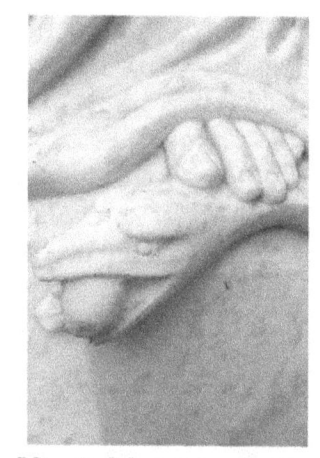 

Left & middle: Virgin Mary stands on snake with apple in its mouth, Right: Acorn on a gated family plot

ANTHEMION (a.k.a. palmette) *Anthemia* is the Greek word for flower. Surprisingly, it's not considered a symbol, but a decorative motif often called a palmette.

APPLE: The apple is most commonly found on the graves of the early Puritans, where the apple was engraved in conjunction with Adam and Eve as a reminder of sin.

B

BASKET OF FLOWERS: When upright, a basket of flowers stands for Hope. When spilled, the strewn blossoms signify grief.

BELLFLOWER In Europe during the Middle Ages and right on through to the Puritans in New England, a funeral procession was led by a person ringing a lytch bell (see lichgates in Chapter 10). Bell-shaped flowers signify mourning and worship due to this connection and resemblance.

BUTTERCUP: Whether growing at the gravesite or engraved on a marker, buttercups signify optimism and a cheery outlook on life.

C

CEDAR: Not only are cedars highly resistant to rot, but many varieties are evergreen. Because of this, cedars have come to symbolize immortality, everlasting faith, and protection from evil.

Since it's often planted in cemeteries, the cedar is nicknamed the "burial tree," and the "funeral tree" in some parts of the USA. There's even a lingering superstition that if you plant a cedar tree, you will die when it grows tall enough to shade your grave. Another folk belief about cedar is that it's bad luck to burn it because Christ's crucifix was made, in part, from cedar.

CHRYSANTHEMUM: Because its blooms continue well into the winter months, the chrysanthemum has come to symbolize longevity and completeness.

Left to right: Corn, Daisy, Daffodil (a.k.a. Narcissus)

CORN: When you see an ear of corn on a headstone, you may be standing at the grave of a farmer. It was an old country custom to send sheaves of corn, instead of floral bouquets, to a farmer's family upon his passing.

There is more to the symbolic meaning of corn than simply indicating a person's occupation. In the Bible, the word "corn" is used for grains, in general, and is used symbolically to indicate spiritual goodness. With its many seeds, corn is also a symbol of fertility and rebirth. Like wheat, corn may also be used to indicate a long life, someone who lived a long and fruitful life.

CYCLAMEN: Thanks to its deep roots, the cyclamen is able to survive adverse conditions. Symbolically, a cyclamen stands for the deep and enduring nature of true love, a love that can withstand adversity.

CYPRESS: Even if you don't think you are good at identifying plants, at least one tree you should become familiar with is the Italian cypress tree. It is also called the Mediterranean cypress, Spanish cypress and Tuscan cypress. Because it appears so frequently in graveyards, it is sometimes simply called the "funeral cypress."

Whatever you choose to call it, the Italian cypress is quite easy to recognize. Look for a tall, thin evergreen.

If you spend any time exploring historic country graveyards, you know they can be extremely hard to find, especially the first time you visit. Even today, with our wonderful GPS gizmos and helpful Google Maps, many graveyards lack an actual address. Since the Italian cypress is easy to spot from a distance, seeing one can help you find your way to a cemetery.

As a symbol, the Italian cypress stands for deep mourning, enduring faith, and the ability to resist evil and temptation. Like the cedar, the cross of the crucifixion was made partly from cypress.

D

DAFFODIL: The botanical name for a daffodil is *narcissus*. This beautiful flower is associated with the ancient Greek myth of Narcissus, the young man who became so in love with his own reflection that he starved to death.

Left to right: Palm frond, Passion flower, Pine cones

Since they are some of the first flowers to bloom each spring, daffodils are a symbol of springtime and are the birth flower for those born in March. Symbolic meanings for the daffodil include: new life, youth (so possibly connected to someone who died young), innocence, and beauty. In the Victorian Language of Flowers, daffodils are associated with "unrequited love," and "deep regard."

DAISY: The daisy is most commonly seen on children's graves. As a symbol, it represents simplicity, innocence, the Christ child, and the Virgin Mary. The name "daisy" comes from "day's eye" because this flower blooms in the morning and closes at sunset.

People sometimes create a necklace or headband out of these flowers by tying their stems together. According to folklore, when kids wear these so-called "daisy chains," it keeps them from being abducted by fairies.

DANDELION: When dandelions are engraved on a historic cemetery monument, they represent the bitterness of grief, since dandelion leaves have a bitter flavor.

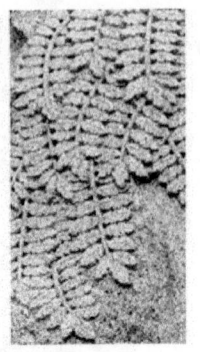

Left to right: Grapevine, Evening primrose, fern

E

EVENING PRIMROSE: The evening primrose is so-called because this flower only blooms at night. To identify an evening primrose on a cemetery engraving, look for a simple-looking flower with four petals. Symbolically, the evening primrose represents undying love, youth, and eternal memory.

EVERGREENS, in general: Even if you don't know the exact species, you may notice a wide variety of evergreen trees in cemeteries. This could even account for the reason why so many burial grounds are named Evergreen, as I mentioned earlier.

Evergreens such as holly, ivy, and yew, cedars, pine trees are associated with immortality, because rather than lose their leaves each fall, they stay green all year, and in this way they symbolize the eternal nature of the soul.

F

FERN: Since ferns often grow in shady places rather than out in the bright light of the sun, they are associated with humbleness, seclusion, and sincerity.

G

GOURDS: Various gourds, such as pumpkins and squash, may be seen in the borders on graves of the earliest New England settlers of the 17th and 18th century as a symbol for how the church and spiritual striving nourish the soul.

GRAPES AND GRAPEVINE: In ancient Egypt, grapes symbolized the heart because the overall shape of a bunch of grapes looks like a heart, and when squeezed, they have a red color, like blood.

Later, the grapes and a grapevine became a symbol to Christians for the blood of Christ. It's also a reference to the biblical passage John, 15:5, which reads, "I am the vine, you are the branches."

GRAPE BUNDLES WITH WHEAT: When a bundle of grapes is shown along with strands of wheat, the grapes represent the blood of Christ, and the wheat symbolizes his body, just as the wine and wafer do in the Christian ceremony of Holy Communion.

H

HOLLY: Like other evergreens, holly symbolizes everlasting life, while its poisonous berries are a reminder of death. In addition, holly symbolizes foresight.

In American folklore, people thought planting holly at their grave would protect their tombstone from lightning strikes.

Left to right: Ivy, Iris, Lotus (a.k.a. water lily)

I

IRIS: The reed-like stems of this plant are a biblical reference to Moses being found among the bullrushes. The iris symbolizes hope, as well as the sorrows of the Virgin Mary.

IVY: Ivy is a common sight in cemeteries, whether depicted on gravestones or actually growing there. Like other evergreens, ivy leaves symbolize immortality. Because of the way they cling to things, ivy vines symbolize everlasting love, eternal friendship, and the idea that while a loved one may be gone, they are not forgotten.

L

LAUREL: As a symbol, laurel leaves stand for life everlasting, victory, and chastity. The link to eternal life is because laurel leaves are slow to decay once they've been picked. The association with victory is because the ancient Romans crowned athletes, poets and warriors with a wreath of laurel leaves. As for the connection to chastity, this is simply because the laurel was the botanical attribute for the Vestal Virgins, Roman priestesses who, rather like nuns, took vows of chastity.

  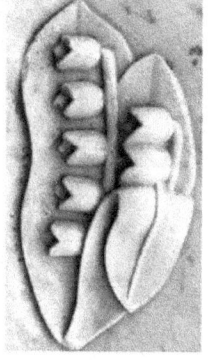

Left to right: Easter lily, Calla lily, Lily of the Valley

LILY: You've probably heard folks refer to someone as having a "lily white reputation." Lilies are not only white, but they symbolize purity. That's why being "lily white" means you are as clean and chaste as possible. The Victorians were especially fond of lilies, and used them to symbolize purity, mercy, innocence and chastity.

Lilies are associated with funeral bouquets due to a longstanding belief that the soul regains its innocence upon death. On a headstone, lilies often refer to the soul's return to a state of purity and innocence in the afterlife. This belief may come from the legend that as Eve cried in the Garden of Eden, feeling repentant for her sinful acts, the first lily grew.

In cemetery statuary, Joseph is sometimes shown holding a lily branch to represent the virginity of his wife, Mary.

In France, lilies were once an emblem of royalty. The decorative motif that we now know as the fleur-de-lis is a stylized lily, with three petals to symbolize the Holy Trinity.

CALLA LILY: Calla lilies stand for purity and holiness, and often signify marriage.

EASTER LILY: Easter lilies represent purity and resurrection. They are frequently associated with Jesus, Mary, Joseph and St Anthony of Padua (See Chapter 13.)

LILY OF THE VALLEY: According to legend, the Virgin Mary's tears turned into lilies of the valley when she cried during Christ's crucifixion. As a cemetery symbol, the lily of the valley stands for purity, virginity, rebirth, innocence and renewal.

LOTUS: Like other members of the illy family, the lotus (a.k.a. water lily) symbolizes purity and innocence. In addtion, it also stands for divine femininity, and spiritual revelation.

The lotus is also a sacred flower to Buddhists. In Buddhism, the lotus bud stands for human potential. If shown with eight petals, it stands for cosmic harmony. If shown with an abundance of petals, it stands for spiritual revelations.

M

MARIGOLD: Despite it's cheery yellow and/or orange hues, "Mary's gold" symbolizes the sorrows of the Virgin Mary, and is therefore considered to symbolize grief. (See Chapter 8, for the marigold's symbolic meaning to Mexican Americans.)

MISTLETOE: Since mistletoe both blooms and produces white berries in midwinter, it is used to symbolize perseverance and strength over adversity.

MORNING GLORY: The morning glory symbolizes the dawning of a new day in the afterlife, as well as youth and new love.

MULBERRY: In the language of flowers and trees the mulberry simply means, "I did not survive you." Also, due to the nature of the silkworm, they are yet another reference to transformation and resurrection.

MYRTLE: The myrtle tree is used to symbolize peace and undying love.

Left to right: Oak leaves & acorns, wreath with poppies

O

OAK TREE AND LEAVES: (See: Acorn) Oak leaves and acorns adorn many tombstones in historic cemeteries in the USA. Oak trees are appreciated and admired for their many special qualities. Not only were they voted America's favorite tree, but in 2004, the U.S. Congress signed a bill making the Oak America's National Tree.

So what makes the oak tree so special to Americans? For one thing, the oak is the most widespread hardwood tree in the USA, with over 60 different species growing throughout the nation.

Specific oak trees have played major roles at pivotal points in United States history. On his way to the Battle of New Orleans, Andrew Jackson camped out beneath Louisiana's Sunnybrook Oaks.

In Texas, Greenwood Memorial Park is home to the Turner Oak, which is not only a Bicentennial Tree, but played a major role in the founding of Fort Worth thanks to gold buried beneath it! The United States Armed Forces even uses oak leaf clusters to denote acts of valor.

The fact that oak trees mature slowly symbolically reminds us how great strength and power can be achieved through patience and faith. Oak trees symbolize: longevity, humble beginnings, patience, faith, power, endurance, and strength.

OLIVE TREE OR BRANCH: Olive branches have become a well-known symbol for peace, but most of us are unaware that this comes from an ancient Greek belief that waving an olive branch around could chase away evil spirits. The olive branch is also a symbol for forgiveness and humility.

P

PALM: When a palm frond is shown in the hand of a saint, it refers to martydom. It is also a way of telling us that the deceased has been rewarded with eternal peace. Seen on its own, a palm frond symbolizes victory over death, and triumph over adversity.

PANSY: The word "pansy" comes from the French word *pensée*, meaning "thought." As a symbol, the pansy refers to meditation and remembrance through keeping loved ones in your thoughts and prayers.

PASSION FLOWER: The passion flower is named for the passion of Christ. With the circular features in the middle of the blossom symbolizing the crown of thorns he wore, and the ten petals representing the ten apostles who remained faithful to him throughout his crucifixion. As a symbol, it represents the soul's redemption through great trials.

Left to right: Palm frond, Passion flower, Pine cones

PINE TREES AND PINE CONES: Like other evergreens such as holly, ivy, and yew, pine trees are associated with immortality. Rather than lose their leaves each fall, pine trees stay green all year long, and in this way they symbolize the eternal nature of the soul. As for the pine cone, like corn, it is considered a fertility symbol because it holds the seeds of the plant.

POPPY: The poppy flower, from which the powerful sedative opium is derived, has long been associated with eternal sleep.

Since World War One, red poppies have become associated with war veterans and those who have lost their life in battle thanks to John McCrae's 1915 poem, "In Flanders Fields" which reads in part, "In Flanders fields the poppies grow, Between the crosses, row on row."

POPLAR: Poplar trees require little care and have strong roots, so they symbolize an independent spirit. Because wind rustling through a poplar's leaves sounds a bit like people whispering, poplars also symbolize how memories of the deceased continue through the conversations of those who love them.

PINEAPPLE: The pineapple was an exotic fruit that early New England missionaries brought back from Hawaii as an impressive souvenir. Pineapples are often seen as a decorative motif on 18th and 19th century American mansions, where they symbolize wealth and prosperity. In the cemetery, they also signify hospitality and eternal life.

Roses often have 3 leaves for the Holy Trinity. Roses with thorns (like the one on the right), are rare.

R

ROSE: Not only do roses represent earthly passion (just think how many are given at Valentine's Day) but they also stand for heavenly perfection.

When carved on a headstone, roses nearly always have three leaves, this is to represent the holy trinity: Father, Son, and Holy Spirit. Roses are rarely shown with thorns, as well. This is a reference to the Virgin Mary, who is sometimes called "the rose with out thorns."

Because of this connection to Mother Mary, roses are symbolic shorthand for women, in general, especially mothers.

ROSE BUSHES: In the language of flowers, here is the meaning behind living rose bushes that you may see planted in graveyards:

> **Burgundy Rose:** Stands for beauty, simplicity, and the Virgin Mary.
> **China Rose:** Represents grace.
> **Dog rose:** Symbolic of life's pleasures as well as life's torments.
> **Moss rose:** Stands for beauty and melancholy.
> **Musk rose**: Represents life's fleeting quality.
> **Province rose:** The fullness of life.
> **White rose:** Stands for purity, chasteness and virginity.
> **Wreath of Roses:** Symbolizes virtue and beauty being remembered and rewarded.
> **Yellow Rose:** Represent friendship and joy.

ROSEMARY: Rosemary has long been believed to improve a person's memory. When seen at a grave it stands for remembrance of those who have died. As an evergreen plant, it is also seen as a reminder of the eternal life of the soul.

S

SHAMROCK: Shamrocks often indicate a person of Irish descent, but they may also simply be a reference to the Holy Trinity.

SUNFLOWER: Sunflowers symbolize devotion to the word of god. The sun form represents God's divine light. Sunflowers turn to face the sun throughout the day, which symbolizes how humans struggle to stay on a holy path throughout life. When a sunflower matures, its blossom permanently faces east, just as many early graves do.

Left to right: Tree stone, Tree of Life, Shamrock

T

THISTLE: Since thistles are a symbol for Scotland, they often appear on the graves of people with Scottish ancestry. Thistles may also symbolize earthly sorrow, or defiance in the face of hardships.

TREE OF LIFE: A tree engraved on a tombstone is often meant to represent the Tree of Life. The tree of life symbolizes knowledge, the cycle of life and the enduring love of God for all of creation.

TREE STONES: A cemetery monument resembling a tree or a tree stump is called a tree stone. Tree stones are often used for members of the Woodmen of the World fraternal organization (See Chapter 16.) They may also be used to symbolize the Tree of Life.

The smaller the tree stone, the younger the deceased. A tiny stump with two clipped branches to represent the parents may be used to mark the grave of a young child.

V

VIOLET: Violets symbolize someone who is quiet, shy and humble.

W

WEEPING WILLOW: As you may have guessed from the name, weeping willows are associated with grief and mourning.

During the Victorian Era, the weeping willow became an extremely common graveyard symbol. It is one of many symbols the Victorians borrowed from ancient Greece. In Greek mythology, weeping willows are associated with the Underworld, and Orpheus carried a willow branch with him when he traveled there to rescue Eurydice from Hades. In the Bible, grieving Israelites hung their harps on weeping willows beside the waters of Babylon.

Left: Weeping willows, Right: Wreath of olive leaves

WHEAT IN A BUNDLE: In historic cemeteries, a sheaf of wheat (often shown in a tidy bundle with a scythe) is usually only seen on the graves of those who have lived for at least 70 years.

You don't have to visit many historic cemeteries for the statistics of life expectancy then-and-now to hit home. It's one thing to read that infant mortality in the United States of America was 90% higher 100 years ago than it is now. It's quite another experience, however, to walk through a historic cemetery in a town that was hit by an epidemic and see a section full of grave markers for children under 6-years-old.

For that reason, I am always happy to see a sheaf of wheat on a headstone. A bundle of wheat represents someone who lived to a ripe old age before their soul's divine harvest.

WHEAT STALKS: If the headstone features a few stalks of wheat that aren't bundled up, there is a different meaning. You may be looking at the grave for someone of Ukranian descent. This is because wheat is one of the symbols for the Ukraine, and represents how the Ukraine is the bread basket for Europe.

Bundles of wheat often indicate a long life

WHEAT STALKS WITH GRAPES AND/OR A CHALICE: Symbolizes the Eucharist, a.k.a. Holy Communion, a Christian ceremony honoring the Last Supper of Christ and his disciples.

WREATHS: The circular shape of a wreath stands for eternal memory and immortality. Ancient Greeks and Romans often crowned award winning poets, athletes, and soldiers with wreaths, so they also symbolize victory. As a graveyard symbol, wreaths stand for victory over death.

    Wreath of Roses: A wreath made of roses celebrates virtue and beauty, as well as heavenly bliss.

    Laurel wreaths: Triumph over death.

Y

YEW: Yew trees have long been connected with churches and burial grounds. The ancient Celts worshipped yew trees and planted them at holy sites. In Britain, early Christians often built their churches in yew groves.

Since yew trees are evergreens and are exceedingly long-lived, they symbolize the eternal life of the soul. They are also associated with mourning, possibly due to the simple fact that they are so commonly seen in cemeteries.

15 SO MANY CROSSES!

With nearly 300 different variations, a person could easily write an entire book on the topic of crosses and the history for each one. Here are some of the most common kinds of crosses that you will encounter in the historic graveyards of America.

Crosses may be depicted several ways. When covered in ivy, they represent the Christian faith and enduring friendship, perhaps someone who is clingy in the nicest possible way. A cross with a serpent twining around it is symbolic of a faithful person's triumph over evil.

Because the same cross may have been used by several different groups to represent different ideas over the centuries, each of these crosses has more than one name.

CRUCIFIX VS CROSS

It should be noted that there is a difference between a crucifix and a cross. The crucifix includes the tormented body of Jesus nailed to the cross, while a cross does not.

1. AGONY CROSS

Each end of the Agony Cross, (aka Cross of Suffering, Pointed Cross) comes to sharp points which symbolize the suffering of Christ.

2. ANCHOR CROSS

Quick Guide to Crosses:

1. Agony Cross

2. Anchor Cross

3. Botonee Cross

4. Calvary Cross

5. Celtic Cross

6. Eastern Cross

7. Glory Cross

8.Greek Cross

9. Ionic Cross

10. Labarum

11. Latin Cross

12. St Andrew's Cross

13. St Peter's Cross

14. Tau Cross

15. Triple Tau Cross

16. Cross Pattee

The Anchor Cross comes in several variations, but what

each of them have in common is that they are stylized anchor designs. The anchor was a secret sign used by early Christians to identify each other during times of persecution.

Crosses(left to right): Agony, Anchor, Botonee

3. BOTONEE CROSS
The Botonee Cross has a trefoil at each end to signify the Holy Trinity.

4. CALVARY CROSS
The Calvary Cross is a Latin cross, flanked by three steps. These steps stand for hope, faith and charity.

5. CELTIC CROSS
The Celtic Cross features a distinctive circle, called a nimbus. Depending on the sourse, this circle symbolizes either the union of heaven and earth or the union of the moon and earth. Often seen on graves of those with Irish descent.

Crosses: Calvary/Botonee mix, Celtic, & Latin on stones

6. EASTERN CROSS:

The foot rest at the bottom of an Eastern Cross (aka Greek Orthodox Cross) is tilted: This is a symbolic way of expressing that the "wise thief" who was crucified on the right side of Christ went to heaven, while the unrepentant thief who was crucified on his left side went to hell.

7. GLORY CROSS

A Glory Cross depicts the rays of God's glory emanating from its center. It's also called the Rayed Cross.

8. GREEK CROSS

If you're familiar with the emblem for the Red Cross, then you already know what a Greek Cross looks like. This type of cross dates back to ancient Egypt. It is a simple looking cross with arms that are all the same size.

As a Christian symbol, the four equal sides representing the four elements: earth, air, water, and fire.

9. IONIC CROSS

Each arm of an Ionic Cross flares out at the end.

10. LABARUM

Also called the "Chi Ro," this cross combines the first two letter of Christ's name using the Greek letters *chi* and *rho*. Long before the Latin Cross became such a well-known symbol for Christianity, the Labarum was the main symbol.

Crosses: Glory crosses

11. LATIN CROSS

The Latin Cross is also called the Protestant Cross because it focuses on Christ as the Risen Savior of mankind rather than his suffering during the crucifixion.

12. ST ANDREW'S CROSS

St Andrew's Cross (aka X-cross, or saltire cross) It is shaped like an X. When St. Andrew was crucified, it is claimed that he requested to be crucified on an X-shaped cross because he did not feel worthy enough to be crucified in the same manner as Christ.

13. ST PETER'S CROSS

St. Peter's cross is so-named because this saint did not feel worthy enough to be crucified in the same manner as Christ. Thanks to modern horror films, people often assume that St. Peter's cross is a Satanist's symbol representing the desire to embrace evil. In a Christian context, it is simply meant to represent St. Peter, and is often shown with a set of keys (which is another symbol associated with him.)

Crosses: Ionic, Labarum, Latin with a palm frond

14. TAU CROSS

Although this style of cross dates back to ancient Egypt, where it was a symbol for immortality, it gets its name because it looks like the Hebrew letter *tau*, which also means "cross." Since it's the last letter in the Hebrew alphabet, it is also used to symbolize immortality and the fulfillment of God's word.

15. TRIPLE TAU CROSS

This unusual looking cross is often incorporated into Masonic imagery. It consists of three Tau Crosses joined together.

16. CROSS PATTEE

Like an Ionic Cross, a Cross Pattée (also called a "cross formée," or "cross patty") has arms that flare out towards the end. The main difference is that the arms are the same length on all four sides. In historic American cemeteries, the Cross Pattée is used to create the Southern Cross of Honor.

Cross Pattee, Southern Cross of Honor, Handmade cross.

The Southern Cross of Honor: During the Civil War, the Congress of the Confederate States created a military decoration to honor Confederate soldiers.

Called the Southern Cross of Honor, this medal depicts a Confederate battle flag flanked by a laurel wreath on top of a cross pattee. The front of the medal reads "The Southern Cross of Honor," while the back reads, *Deo Vindice*, which translates from Latin to mean, "With God as our protector."

In historic graveyards, a metal version of the Southern Cross of Honor may be found beside the grave of a Confederate soldier. These crosses have usually been placed there by historical heritage clubs such at the Sons of Confederate Veterans, or the Daughters of the Confederacy. Both of these groups require members to be directly descended from Confederate soldiers who served honorably. Other names for this marker include the "Iron Cross of Honor," and the "SVC Iron Cross."

The Southern Cross of Honor can also be seen as an engraving at the top of Confederate tombstones issued by the U.S. Department of Veterans.

16 CLUBS, SECRET SOCIETIES & ORGANIZATIONS

P rivate social clubs were once extremely popular in the United States. By the 1920's, roughly half of all citizens belonged to at least one fraternal organization. Many people belonged to three or four.

The hey day for America's private clubs was during its biggest immigration surge, the years right after the Civil War through the 1920's. By the late 1800's, there were more than 2000 groups from which to choose. Some had specific charitable goals, but many existed simply for drinking and having fun. The Exalted Order of Big Dogs (OEBD), for instance, was a club for musicians weighing at least 200 pounds. In keeping with the canine-theme, they called their meeting halls "dog kennels."

Other lighthearted fraternal orders included the Ancient Order of Mutts, Bagmen of Bagdad, Concatenated Order of Hoo-Hoo, Exalted Order of Big Dogs, Fraternal Order of Reindeer, Knownothingism, Mystic Order of Veiled Prophets of the Enchanted Realm, Order of Bugs, and the Order of Regenerated Franks- among many others.

Most fraternal societies, however, were popular because they provided helpful services to their members. Some offered life insurance, medical care and help with funeral expenses. Before Social Security and other government social services, it made sense to join as many of these clubs as you could afford. Although the bulk of these clubs offered membership to men only, many also offered a companion group for women.

Some fraternal organizations, such as the Odd Fellows and the Masons, had cemeteries for their members. Others, like the Woodmen of the World , provided a tombstone for members. Although this benefit was phased out over time, it was a powerful draw in the late 1800's, and Woodmen of the World's unique tree stone monuments are some of the most eye-catching markers you will see in historic graveyards throughout the south. Other fraternal organizations granted members space in opulent mausoleums.

While it's beyond the scope of this book to include every single emblem from each of these groups, here are some of the most common ones you will come across in historic graveyards of the USA.

AMERICAN LEGION: The American Legion was stablished in 1919 and is still going strong as of this writing. Its primary goal is to care for ex-servicemen, especially the disabled and elderly.

The background of the American Legion emblem represents the rays of the sun, and symbolizes how the power of the group will chase off the dark influences violence and evil. The wreath stands for the memory of those who have lost their lives in combat, that their sacrifice will never be forgotten.

BOY SCOUTS OF AMERICA: The Boy Scouts of America was founded 1910 to teach outdoor skills and promote good character and public service. The club is still going strong and even though I don't often see its emblem on a tombstone, I've seen it on commemorative plaques after a scout troop has cleaned and restored a historic cemetery.

The Boy Scouts of America emblem consists of a fleur-de-lis with an eagle and a shield. The emblem often includes a knot at the bottom which is meant to remind members to "do a good turn daily."

DAUGHTERS OF REBEKAH: The Daughters of Rebekah was created in 1851 as a companion group to the International Order of Odd Fellows.

The Daughters of Rebekah features the letters "d" and "r" superimposed on each other to the left, a crescent moon facing them on the right, and an olive branch bearing dove in the middle. On a tombstone, this emblem may also include a beehive, a sprinkling of seven stars, and/or a lily flower.

According to the club's literature, the moon and stars symbolize the consistent order of God and nature. The lily stands for purity, the beehive for the value of working together, and the dove for peace.

DAUGHTERS OF THE AMERICAN REPUBLIC (DAR): Daughters of the American Republic, another women's only group, was established in 1890. The only way to be accepted as a member of DAR is to have direct lineage to to an ancestor who sided with the colonies to achieve independence from England during the American Revolution. The DAR is a deeply patriotic club.

Besides proving the genetic 'pedigree' needed to become a member of DAR, a woman must also prove herself to be "personally acceptable" to the group. Membership today numbers somewhere around 180,000, with chapters all over the world.

According to the Daughters of the American Revolution Handbook, the golden wheel is a spinning wheel, the stars surrounding it represent the original 13 American colonies, and the plant poking out at the top and bottom is flax.

Left to right: Royal Arch Mason, Masonic G, Daughters of the American Revolution, 33rd Degree Mason

DAUGHTERS OF THE REPUBLIC OF TEXAS: Created in 1891, the Daughters of the Republic of Texas was originally known at the Daughters of the Lone Star. Membership is open to women who can prove lineage to ancestors who served the Republic of Texas, before its statehood in 1836.

The group is still around and is very active in historic preservation throughout Texas. Its emblem features a single star (representing the Republic of Texas) surrounded by lived branches to signify peace.

ELKS (BPOE): Elks (BPOE) The Benevolent Protective Order of Elks was founded in 1868 as a way to skirt the blue laws of New York, which prohibited the sale of booze on Sundays. Since then, the Elks have become much more than a mere drinking club. Membership currently tops over one million.

According to the club's brochure, their mascot was chosen because the elk is a uniquely American animal that works together in a herd, and while strong enough to protect itself, it does not seek out violence without provocation.

The Elks' emblem features an elk superimposed over the face of a clock with a single star at the top and the letters BPOE around the edge. The antlers symbolize protection, and the star stands for fidelity.

On the Elks Club emblem, the hands of the clock are always set at 11:00, because at this time of night, members drink a special toast to members who have passed away.

Left to right: The clock on the Elks Club tumulus is always 11pm, Grand Master Mason emblem

FEDERATION OF EAGLES (FOE): Originally called "The Order of Good Things," the Federation of Eagles was founded by a group of Seattle theater owners in 1898. At first, the group was solely comprised of actors, stagehands and others associated with the theater business. Because of their nomadic nature, the group quickly spread throughout America.

Like many other clubs of this era, the FOE provided health insurance. They even had club-appointed physicians so members could get quality health care. In addition to funeral benefits, the FOE provided a script for funeral services as an additional benefit to members.

A tombstone for an Eagles' club member may simply have the letters "FOE" engraved on the marker. They may also have the club's emblem, which features a bald eagle, surrounded by the letters "FOE."

Left to right: Modern Woodmen of America, Knights Templar, Knights of Pythias, Shriners

FREEMASONS: While many groups created during America's hey day for fraternal organizations called themselves the "Ancient Order" of one thing or the other, the Ancient Free and Accepted Masons (a.k.a. Freemasons or simply, Masons) can truly lay claim to such a lofty title since the earliest known mention of the group dates back to 1390!

COMPASS AND SQUARE:

Masonic emblems featuring a compass and a carpenter's square with the letter "G" in the middle are a common sight in cemeteries old and new. The carpenter's square stands for morally correct behavior, while the compass signifies keeping your desires in check. The G in the middle of the emblem stands for Gnosis (the Greek word for knowledge), Generations (as in passing your knowledge down through the ages), and God (who is the grand architect of the universe.)

While the compass and square is the main emblem for the Masons, there are a few other symbols you may see in historic cemeteries.

Left: Masonic pillars, Top: 32nd & 33rd Degree Masons Bottom: Grand Master Mason, Black & white checkered floor stands for struggle between light & dark.

DOUBLE HEADED EAGLE: Masonic headstones may also feature an emblem known as the Double-headed Eagle of Lagash, an ancient symbol dating back over 2000 years. On a tombstone, this emblem means the deceased was affiliated with a branch of the Masons known as the Scottish Rite.

Symbolically, the two-headed eagle represents mankind's dual nature as both a physical and a spiritual being, who must choose good over evil. The Latin phrase *spes mea in doe est* below the eagle, means "My hope is in God."

HTWSSTKS: The graves for some Masons will feature the letters: HTWSSTKS. This rather puzzling acronym is usually engraved inside a keystone shape, and stands for, "Hiram, Tyrian's Widow's Son, Sent to King Solomon."

Third degree Freemasons study the tale of a man named Hiram Abiff (a.k.a. Hiram, Tyrian's Widow's Son.) According to legend, Hiram was chief architect for the Temple of King Solomon. When bad guys tried to squeeze the secret masonic passwords out of Hiram, he valiantly refused to tell them. As a result, the bad guys killed poor Hiram. In Masonic teachings, Hiram's story is held up as an example of loyalty.

When you see HTWSSTKS on someone's headstone, you know that not only were they a Royal Arch Mason, but that they made it at least as far as the third degree in that fraternal order.

KNIGHTS OF COLUMBUS (KofC): The Knights of Columbus was created in 1882 as a fraternal organization to assist widows and orphans within the Catholic church. From 1783 until 1983, the Catholic church did not allow its members to join the Masons. Knights of Columbus patterned many of its rituals and degrees after the Freemasons, so much so that some people refer to it as the "Catholic Masons." These days, the organization is mainly an insurance group.

The Knights of Columbus emblem was inspired by the shields use by medieval knights. The top of the shield reads "K of C" for the name of the group. The shield itself features a crossed dagger and anchor, with a fasces bundled around an axe in the middle. The anchor here refers to the mariner Christopher Columbus, for whom the club is named, while daggers were commonly used by knights. The axe and fasces symbolize authority.

Left to right: Eastern Star, Eastern Star, Woodmen of the World, Supreme Forest Woodmen Circle

KNIGHTS OF PYTHIAS (KP): The Knights of Pythias was created in 1864 as a secret society for government clerks. Some sources claim that this group uses more than 20,000 different symbols, so you will see quite a variety on headstones rather than one easily identifiable emblem.
Even so, a knight's helmet surrounded by the letters F, B and C (for Friendship, Benevolence, and Charity), you're probably looking at an emblem for the Knights of Pythias.

A skull and crossbones is sometimes included in the motif, but it's not mandatory. When a triangular shield is included, it represents the Holy Trinity. When you see a Knights of Pythias emblem featuring a long sword lying on the Bible it stands for religious faith and the law. A falcon sometimes appears on top of the knight's helmut to symbolize vigilance.

KNIGHTS TEMPLAR: The Knights Templar are one of several masonic offshoots. According to legend, the Knights Templar were created in 1118 by a group of warrior monks who patrolled the roads near Jerusalem to keep religious pilgrims safe on their journeys.

Along the way, these monks became so wealthy that in 1307, the French King Phillipe le Bel attacked them and seized their riches. Although many Knights Templar were slain, a few made it to England, Scotland, and Portugal.

While in exile, the legend continues, these survivors created the Freemasons.

Beyond that, it's a rather hazy picture. In historic graveyards, however, the emblem for the Knights Templar can occasionally be found in conjunction with York Rite masons.

The Knights Templar emblem features a cross and a crown inside a cross with wide flared arms, and often included the Latin phrase *in hoc signo vinces*, meaning, "In this sign you shall conquer."

LIONS CLUB: Established in 1917, the Lions Club is a service club that helps communities by raising money for worthwhile charities. The name of the club itself, serves as an acronym, meaning: Liberty, Intelligence, Our Nation's Safety.

The Lions Club emblem consists of the letter L between the heads of two lions. The lions face opposite directions to represent a member of the club looking back on their past with satisfaction and towards the future with confidence as they continue to serve their community. The word "Lions" is often written along the top.

MASONS: Masons (see Freemasons, above)

MOOSE (LOOM): Like so many other fraternal organizations, the Loyal Order of the Moose (LOOM) began as a drinking club for men.

Although the group was established in 1888, membership didn't really boom until they added insurance benefits. After that, members could spend $5 or $10 a year for a policy that gave benefits to their wives and children if members became disabled or died.

The Moose club emblem may or may not feature the

head of a moose. It usually included the acronym "PAP," standing for "Purity, Aid, Progress."

International Order of Odd Fellows symbols

ODD FELLOWS (IOOF): The Independent Order of Odd Fellows was established in England during the 1700's, so like the Masons, its traditions go back quite a ways. What makes Odd Fellows odd is that their charity and benevolence could make them seem odd when compared to others.

The Odd Fellows are sometimes called the "Three Link Fraternity" because its main symbol is a three-linked chain. This chain may or may not contain the letters F, L, and T, for Friendship, Love, and Truth.

One reason Odd Fellows graves are a common sight in historic graveyards is that not only were members offered death benefits, but each time a new club was established, members would create a new cemetery in that town, or at least purchase a large number of plots in the local burial ground for club members.

ORDER OF THE EASTERN STAR (OES): The Order of the Eastern Star was created in 1849 to be the women's auxiliary to the Masons. These days, however, the group accepts both men and women as members.

The Eastern Star emblems features a five-pointed star

inside of which each arm you will see a symbol. Each of these symbols represents one of the five Biblical heroines as they fulfill the many different roles that a woman can have

throughout her life:

Adah- daughter: Adah is symbolized by a veil and the story of her self-sacrifice is used to teach duty and obedience.

Ruth - widow: A sheaf of wheat stands for Ruth, a widow who gathered wheat. The lesson here is that small acts of kindness and patience accumulate into something larger over time.

Esther - wife: Esther was a Jewish women who was chosen to be the queen of Persia. She is symbolized by a crown, and the lesson she passes along is that of being faithful to family and friends.

Martha - sister: The sister of Lazarus, Martha is symbolically depicted with a broken column. Lessons surrounding her involve faith in God and belief in eternal life.

Electa - mother: A chalice is the item chosen to represent Electa, the final Biblical heroine included within the star. The lesson associated with her involves generosity and hospitality.

SHRINERS: Although the full name for this organization is actually the Imperial Council of the Ancient Arabic Order of the Nobles of the Mystic Shrine, most of us know this group as Shriners.

Like the Knights Templar, this group has connections to the Masons. In fact, when the group was established in 1872, membership was open only to men who had already become 32nd Degree Master Masons and were part of the

Left to right: Knights of Pythias, Woodmen of the World tree stone, non-Woodmen of the World tree stone

Knights Templar. While Masons are often perceived as serious and secretive, Shriners have an overtly playful side. They are often seen at public parades wearing silly outfits. I once saw a dozen fez-wearing Shriners riding tiny motorbikes. As if that wasn't enough, these men were dressed in white jumpsuits and pompadours a la Elvis!

This public propensity for goofiness did not always impress the Masons, who once considered banning Shriners from their ranks. It's probably no accident that the first letters in the phrase "Ancient Arabic Order of the Nobles of the Mystic Shrine" can be rearranged to spell "a Mason."

The Shriners' emblem depicts a scimitar from which dangles a crescent shape that surrounds a five-pointed star. The scimitar symbolizes the members of the organization. The two sides of the crescent contain claws, which are meant to represent philanthropy and fraternity. The star stands for the children who are helped through the generosity of the Shriners each year. Some engravings is include a sphinx (meant to signify the governing body of the club) along with the Latin phrase *robur et furor*, meaning "strength and fury."

WOODMEN OF THE WORLD: Some of the most eye-catching monuments you will see in historic graveyards through the South are those erected to honor members of the Woodmen of the World, a fraternal order established in 1890 by a man named Joseph Cullen Root.

In its earliest days, Woodmen of the World membership was restricted to white men between the ages of 18 and 45, except for those employed in particularly dangerous occupations such as gunpowder factory employees and even bartenders. The club offered health insurance and death benefits to its members, including a uniquely styled cemetery monument. The bigger your policy, the bigger this tree-shaped marker would be.

In historic cemeteries, these tree-shaped markers can be spotted from quite a distance and are often a good way to tell where the oldest graves will be found.

While the original group was called Woodmen of the World, there are several splinter groups, if you'll pardon the pun, including Modern Woodmen of America (MWA), Women of Woodcraft (WOW), and Neighbors of Woodcraft (NOW.)

Symbolically, these tree stones represent knowledge and life. The severed branches represent a life cut short, while the axe, sledge and wedge stand for the works of man. Other symbols often included on a Woodmen of the World tree stone include doves for peace, lilies for purity, and ivy for friendship.

17 COMMON LATIN PHRASES

Just as you learn a lot about ancient Greece if you spend time in historic graveyards, you'll also pick up a smattering of Latin. Here are a few common phrases and abbreviations. While these are most common in Catholic graveyards, you will find some in Protestant burial grounds, as well:

ad patres: To the fathers (who have passed away.)

agnus dei: The lamb of God.

anno aetatis sua (AAS) In the year of his/her age

anno Domini (AD) - in the year of our Lord

annos vixit (av) S/he lived (followed by the amount of years.)

beatae memoriae: (BM) Of blessed memory

Dei gratia: By the grace of God

Dei gratias: Thanks be to God

Deo, Optimo, Maximo (DOM): This is the motto of the Benedictine Order of monks, meaning: to God, the Best, the Greatest.

Domino, Optimo, Maximo (DOM): The Benedictine motto is also sometimes translated as this: The Lord, the Best, the Greatest.

dum tacet clamat: Though silent, he speaks. (This is seen most commonly on the graves of Woodmen of the World.)

gloria in excelsis deo: Glory be to God, the most high

hic iacet (HI): Here lies.

hic iacet sepultus (HIS): Here lies buried.

hic sepultus (HS): Here is buried.

Ici repose: Here rests.

Iesus Nazarenus, Rex Iudaeorum (INRI): Jesus Christ, King of the Jews.

In hoc signo spes mea: In this sign (the cross) is my hope.

in hoc signos vinces: By this sign (the cross) you shall conquer.

Iesus Nazarenus, Rex Iudaeorum (INRI): Jesus of Narareth, King of the Jews.

IHS: Iota, eta, and sigma are the first three letters of Jesus when spelled with the Greek alphabet. When IHS is used on its own it is type of abbreviation called a Christogram. Sometimes all three letters are engraved one on top of the other so that the end result looks a bit like a modern dollar sign.

IHS originated as a Christogram, but over the centuries people have assigned other meanings to these three letters. The most popular ones are: *in hoc salus* for "there is safety in this," *in hoc signo* meaning "by this sign," and, *Iesus hominum salvator*, for "Jesus, the savior of mankind."

memento mori: Remember you must die.

obit (ob): S/he died.

Pax (PX): Peace.

Resurgam: I shall rise again.

Spes mes in deo est: - My hope is in God.

Verbi dei minister (VDM): Minister of God's word.

requiescat in pace (RIP): May s/he rest in peace.

Taus deo: God be praised.

Tempus erat: Time has run out. (Often shown with an engraving of an hour glass to really drive the point home.)

Verbi dei minister (VDM): Minister of the word of god. (Used to indicate that the deceased was a minister. The Latin phrase *verbi divini minister* (meaning "minister of the divine word") may also be used.

18 MISC. CEMETERY SYMBOLS FROM A TO Z

In this section of the book, you will find an A to Z listing of cemetery symbols that didn't fit into the specific categories described in the other chapters.

ALPHA AND OMEGA: Alpha is the first letter of the Greek alphabet, and Omega is the last. The two letters are sometimes engraved with one on top of the other. Sometimes Alpha will be engraved on one side of a tomb and Omega on the other. Symbolically, these letters represent God, creator of the beginning, the end, and everything in between.

ANCHOR: While anchors sometimes appear on the graves of sailors, surprisingly, this is the exception, not the rule. In a seaside community an *upside down* anchor on a headstone may signify that the deceased lost their life at sea.

More frequently, however, the anchor is a Christian symbol representing faith set in strong foundations. Like the fish. The anchor was a secret symbol for persecuted Christians. In fact, the Anchor Cross was created during the time of Roman persecution (See Chapter 15.)

When an anchor is held by a female, it's your clue that she is Hope, one of the Seven Virtues (See Chapter 13.)

The Greek letters Alpha & Omega

ANVIL: While this could be on a blacksmith's grave, an anvil also refers to St. Eligius. Also known as Eloy, St. Eligius is the patron saint of blacksmiths. Symbolically, the anvil represents creation by referring to the forging of the universe.

ARCH: Arches and archways symbolize the entrance to Heaven. In Roman times, arches were often built to celebrate military victories, which is why they also represent victory over death as we enter the eternal afterlife.

ARROW: In America, arrows are most commonly seen on graves from the 17th and 18th century graves in New England. They will often be brandished by crudely engraved imps, and may be shown stabbing a skull.

If the arrows accompany a saintly figure, it refers to Saint Sebastian, while three arrows joined together is a symbol for brotherly love and respect.

Left to right: Anchor, Arch, Arrows

AXE: Since the axe was used to clear land across America, it may symbolize the progress of civilization. An axe and maul are often seen together on tree stone monuments for Woodmen of the World (See Chapter 16.)

B

BALLS: Stone balls at a gravesite may simply be meant as a decorative element, however, cannonballs are often used for war monuments and veterans.

When a pedestal is topped by a single polished stone ball, it most likely represents the universe.

Three balls placed directly beside each other, is symbolic shorthand for money. This stems from the legend of St. Nicholas of Myrna (aka Santa Claus) who generously tossed three bags of money into a poor man's house so his daughters would have dowry money. This is also why pawn shops often use the symbol of three balls in their signage.

BAT: Bats are not a common symbol in historic American graveyards, but may be tucked into a decorative edge here and there. As a symbol, they represent the mysterious workings of the underworld.

Axes are a common symbol for Woodmen of the World

BED: By the Victorian Era, the idea of death as "eternal rest" and being "asleep in Jesus" was often expressed by making headstones look like the death bed of the deceased.

Until the 1930's, relatives would sometimes place an actual wood or metal bed frame on a gravesite as a grave good meant to ensure they had a restful sleep in eternity.

BEE: When seen on a historic tombstone, a single bee may symbolize the resurrection of Christ.

It may also signify chastity. A single bee is often shown with the Virgin Mary, as a reference to the virgin birth of Christ. This stems from an ancient belief that bees did not reproduce like other animals. Instead, it was thought that they found their young by foraging through flower blooms.

BEEHIVE: Just as bees work together to make honey, a beehive symbolizes the power and greatness that can be achieved through working together.

A beehive may also indicate membership in the Daughters of Rebekah (See Chapter 16.)

Boats may be symbolic (left) or literal (right)

BELL: A handbell symbolizes grief and mourning. The leader of a Puritan funeral procession rang a special handheld bell called either a "mourning bell" or a "lych bell" (See Chapter 10) on their way to the graveyard to make it known that the person was no longer alive in flesh but only in spirit.

BIBLE: Symbolizes Christian faith. (See: Books.)

BIRD: Generally speaking, birds represent the soul. When flying, they refer to resurrection and the soul's flight to Heaven. (See also: Donve, Pelican, Eagle, Owl.)

BOAT: Maritime symbols are quite common on the American east coast, especially in fishing communities. On modern markers, of course, a boat may simply mean the deceased was a mariner.

In historic cemeteries, however, you often see a boat being guided by the angel of death to symbolize the deceased's final voyage from the land of the living to the land of the dead.

When a boat is shown sailing towards the sun, it represents God guiding this newly departed soul to Heaven.

Books (left to right): Closed, Open with veil, The Bible

BOOKS

BOOK: When books are depicted on a headstone, they can mean several different things. Often, the book is labeled "Bible," so there's no need to guess which book it refers to. Here are some other possibilities to consider when you see a book:

CLOSED BOOK: A closed book may mean a long life lived to the last page. It may also signify that the deceased was a minister, nun, or even a teacher. If you see two or three books in a stack, it may mean the deceased was a Mormon (see below.)

OPEN BOOK: In this case, the person's life was cut short before they reached the last page.

OPEN BOOK WITH DRAPED CLOTH: The cloth represents the veil of death cutting a life short before the final page of the deceased person's life was written.

OPEN BOOK WITH WRITING: This symbolizes the Book of Life.

BOOK WITH A CROWN: The Kingdom of Heaven and the Bible.

Left to right: Beehive, Butterfly, Ball

TWO OR THREE BOOKS: If two, it's most likely the Bible and the Book of Mormon. If three, it's the Bible, the Book of Mormon, and the Doctrine and Covenants.

BUGLE: A bugle looks much like a trumpet, except it lacks the three buttons on top. It also differs from Gabriel's horn because it is much shorter in length. When seen on a headstone, a bugle often indicates military service.

BUTTERFLY: On a modern headstone, this may simply represent a fondness for butterflies. However, symbolically, butterflies represent the resurrection, and the soul's transformation after death. When seen on a young person's monument, they refer to a short life, just as butterflies are beautiful short-lived creatures.

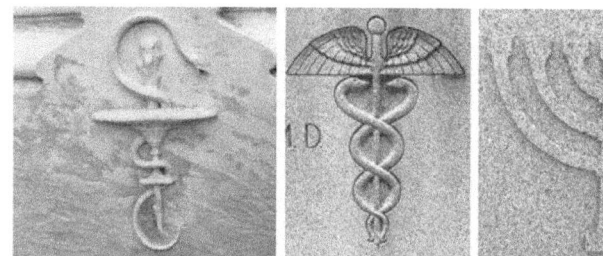

Left to right: Rod of Asclepius, Caduceus, Menorah

C

CADUCEUS: The caduceus is a staff with snakes twining around it and a small pair of wings on top. This symbol dates back to ancient Greek. The caduceus represents Hermes, the ancient messenger between mortals and man.

In 1902, the US Army Medical corps adopted the caduceus as their emblem. It is often used on doctor's headstones.

The ancient Greeks had another staff with a single snake twining around it. This staff is associated with Asclepius, their god of healing and medicine. So even though we now associate the caduceus with medicine, this is due to it being mistaken for the Rod of Asclepius at one point.

CANDLES

CANDLE: Candles may be used to symbolize human mortality. They often represent the divine life of Christ and to symbolize how religious faith can provide your soul with light even through the darkest of times.

In Jewish cemeteries, a candle on a headstone may simply convey that the deceased was a woman. Here are some other symbolic ideas that candles may represent:

CANDLE BEING SNUFFED: Symbolic of a life cut short.

THREE CANDLES: Symbolizes the Holy Trinity: Father, Son and Holy Spirit.

FOUR CANDLES: The four Evangelists (Matthew, Mark, Luke, John.)

FIVE CANDLES: The five wounds of Christ during his crucifixion.

SIX CANDLES: Refers to the six days it took for God to create the earth (minus the seventh day, when he rested.)

SEVEN CANDLES: A grouping of seven items offers quite a few possible symbolic meanings, including: All seven days of creation, the seven joys and sorrows of the Virgin Mary, the seven deadly sins , and even, perhaps, the sevenfold gifts of the Holy Spirit (this refers to the sun, the moon and the first five planets from the sun.)

MENORAH: The menorah is one of the best-known symbols of Judaism. A menorah is a candelabra symbolizing the Divine Light of God spreading throughout the world. A menorah with seven candles often appears on the grave of a righteous woman, a person who helped to spread the Light of God through her actions.

CANNONS

CANNONS:

UPRIGHT CANNON: In military graveyards, cannons are often posed upright and topped with a cannon ball. A row of these can even be used to create a fence around a monument or grave. By standing upright, such cannons symbolize that the region is now at peace. If the cannon is topped with a flame or fuse, it refers to the soul's eternal flame.

CROSSED CANNONS: Crossed cannons indicate a soldier who served in an artillery unit for the military.

CANNON BALLS: These are often used at the graves of deceased soldiers.

CASTLE: Represents God's strength, the Kingdom of Heaven, and how a person's faith in God can keep them safe. On headstones, castles usually feature three windows to symbolize the Holy Trinity.

CHAINS

CHAINS: Chains can have several meanings. In America, when an actual chain is used to mark a grave it may mean that the deceased was a slave, with each link of the chain representing a year spent in slavery. I have never seen an example of that, however. I have seen the grave of two white men that has a single chain hung between their gravesites.

THREE LINKED CHAIN: In America, the engraving of a three-linked chain often represents a fraternal organization called the Odd Fellows, especially if the links contain the letters FLT (See Chapter 16.)

Cloth with & without fringe, Angel with chalice (right)

A three-linked chain may, however, simply be a reference to the Holy Trinity (Father, Son, Holy Ghost) as groups of three often symbolize.

BROKEN LINKED CHAIN: Sometimes you will see an engraving of God's hand reaching down from the heavens to pluck away one of the links in a chain as a way to symbolize how this person's death is a broken link in the family's connection.

CHAIR: A small empty chair often indicates the death of a child. Most actual seating in graveyards consists of benches, a practice dating back to ancient Greece.

CHECKERED PATTERN: - A black and white checkered pattern may symbolize the struggle between good and evil.

CHI-RO (XP): When you see the letters XP it is an abbreviation for the Greek word for Christ.

CHI-RO INSIDE A WHEEL: Symbolizes the evolution of the spirit.

Broken columns (left & mid), Cube (right)

CHRYSALIS: This symbolizes the transformation of the human soul, from bodily death to spiritual resurrection

CIRCLE: Stands for the family circle, the circle of life, and eternity. Look for circles made from chains, ropes, snakes and other items. If the circle is broken, it represents how the deceased's life has disrupted the family circle.

CLEAVER: A trade symbol for a butcher.

CLOCK: (see also watch) Refers to the passing of time. The time that the clock is set at may refer to the time of death. If the deceased was a member of the Elks club, then the clock will most likely be set for 11:00 p.m. (See Chapter 16.)

CLOTH: Cloth is a frequent motif in historic cemeteries, and is often shown draped over an urn. There is a subtle distinction to be made when observing depictions of cloth in a cemetery.

A fringe on the edge of the cloth symbolizes the veil between life and death, as when people say that someone "saw curtains" as a euphemism for their death.

A clothe with no fringe represents the earthly garments

humans cast aside when leaving this world and going to the next.

CLOUDS: Clouds may be so stylized that you may not recognize them as such at first glance. As a symbol, clouds represent the heavens above.

COLUMN: When not broken, columns represent a noble life. When the column appears broken, it represents a life cut short. (See Chapter 11.)

COAT OF ARMS: A coat of arms is a way to represent a family's historical lineage. You may sometimes be able to piece together the meaning of a family's coat of arms by looking at the individual symbols displayed upon it.

COINS: Symbolically, when the image of coins are engraved on a headstone, it's probably meant to represent charity, or even the idea that, "You can't take it with you." (See Chapter 8.)

COFFIN: Symbolizes death.

COLUMN (BROKEN) A life cut short, usually represents the head of the family.

COMPASS: Alone, a compass may be a vocational symbol for a ship's captain, or a ship builder. When shown with a carpenter's square, it is most likely a Masonic emblem (See Chapter 16.)

CORNUCOPIA: Also called the "horn of plenty," a cornucopia represents life's final harvest at the end of a fruitful life.

CROOK (SHEPHERD'S STAFF): A crook may symbolize charity, which is why it is often seen on the graves of Odd Fellows (See Chapter 16.) It is also refers to Jesus Christ in his role as the Good Shepherd who leads his flock to salvation.

CRANE: Sculptures of cranes may be found in historic graveyards perching on monuments as a symbol of Christ's resurrection, as well as loyalty and vigilance.

According to ancient legends, each night flocks of cranes gather around their leader, just as loyal subjects surround their king. For this reason, cranes symbolize loyalty.

When depicted standing on one leg, cranes symbolize vigilance. This stems from another legend claiming that the crane holds a pebble in the one foot to stay alert. If the bird starts to doze off, it will drop the stone, thereby waking itself up.

CROWN: Saints are often shown wearing crowns to indicated their martyrdom or to show that they descended from royalty. When a crown is seen by itself, or draped on a cross it can refer to victory, leadership, and the Kingdom of Heaven.

CUBE: Many ancient symbols, including the cube, have roots in geometry and math. That might seem odd today, but at one time, math, science and religion were not considered separate pursuits. Even Sir Isaac Newton, the scientific genius most famous for his theory of gravity, had a fascination with sacred geometry.

Newton devoted countless hours attempting to figure out the exact dimension of the Temple of Solomon. Since the Temple of Solomon features prominently in the teachings of the Royal Arch Masons. And while it has not been proven conclusively, many people suspect that Sir Isaac Newton was a mason. So keep in mind that when you see a cube on a historic headstone, there is a chance the deceased was a freemason.

A cube is one of many different symbols associated with sacred geometry. Since it can sit flat on the ground, a cube is associated with the earth. For this reason, as a cemetery symbol a cube represents earth and our earthly existence.

Even the orientation of the cube has a symbolic meaning. When the cube is positioned so that the corners point up and down this refers to the directions of Heaven and earth.

CUP, CHALICE, GOBLET: A cup with a stem (like a wine glass) refers to Christianity's holy sacraments and communion. It may also symbolize how mankind yearns to be filled with Christ's divine teachings.

CURTAIN: (See Cloth)

D

DEER: Deep and enduring religious faith. However, if the animal is actually an elk, then you are most likely looking at the emblem of an Elks club member (See Chapter 16.)

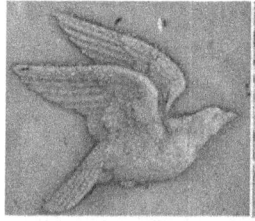  

Dove: Ascending (left), Olive branch (mid), Broken wing (rt)

DICE: On modern graves, a pair of dice may simply mean the deceased enjoyed gambling. On older graves, a pair of dice may be a reference to the Roman soldiers who cast dice to decide which one of them could keep Jesus Christ's garments after his crucifixion.

DOG: (See also Foo Dogs) In many cultures, dogs are believed to have connections to the other side allowing them to roam between the land of the living and of the dead.

Symbolically, these animals represent faithfulness, watchfulness, loyalty, and courage. On modern tombstones, they may represent a specific dog, and will often be the same breed as the one owned by the deceased.

DOLPHIN: Like the fish and anchor, dolphins were another secret symbol for early Christians. Because dolphins have been known to save drowning victims, when seen on headstones, they represent salvation.

DOVES

DOVE: In general, doves represent innocence, peace, and/ or the Holy Spirit. The meaning of a particular dove depends on what it is doing:

DOVE FLYING DOWNWARDS: When a dove is shown flying downwards, it represents the Holy Spirit coming down from heaven.

SEVEN DOVES: A flurry of seven doves on a tombstone represents the seven gifts of the Holy Spirit: wisdom, understanding, counsel, fortitude, knowledge, wonder and piety.

DOVE WITH OLIVE BRANCH: Dove flying downwards refers to the Holy Spirit arriving at Christ's baptism. but the olive branch in its mouth hearkens to ancient Greece.

DOVE HOLDING A GLOBE: If the dove holds the earth in its beak, it's associated with the 4th degree ranking in the Knights of Columbus fraternal organization (See Chapter 16.)

DOVE WITH BROKEN WING: Usually seen on the grave of a young child, with the dove as a symbol of innocence.

DOVE WITH MAIL IN ITS BEAK: In Victorian era graves, a dove with a note in its mouth recalls that some young lovers during that time period sometimes used carrier pigeons to exchange letters.

DRAGON: If seen by itself, a dragon may represent someone of Welsh descent. If the dragon is under attack (by St Michael or St George, for instance) then it stands for evil being triumphed over by the forces of good.

DRAGONFLY: When seen on older tombstones, the dragonfly symbolizes eternal life.

E

EAGLE: The ancient Roman Republic frequently used eagles in its imagery, and since the ancient Greeks and Romans were such an influence on American's founding fathers. it's one of the reasons we chose the bald eagle as our national symbol, and not the wild turkey, as Benjamin Franklin had proposed.

Eagles are also associated with St. John (See Chapter 13.) Eagles are often seen flying high in the sky, which is why symbolically, they may represent the ability to triumph over lower forces.

In nature, eagles are at the top of the food chain. So to humans, they seemed like the king of all birds. This is how they came to be associated with royalty.

In some Native American traditions, the bald eagle is a messenger between God and man. Its feathers, to them, represent the sun's rays and the Great Spirit.

EAGLE WITH TWO HEADS: A two-headed eagle is the emblem of the32nd degree of the Scottish Rite of Fremasonry (See Chapter 16.)

EUCHARIST: The combination of a chalice with grapes, wheat and a wafer is called the Holy Eucharist. On tombstones, this symbol may indicate that the deceased was a minister.

EX VOTO: If you come across a small room with a wall hung with miniature replicas of arms, eyes, and legs, you have most likely walked into a chapel full of ex votos.

An ex voto is a way of asking either God or a particular saint for spiritual assistance and/or giving thanks for prayers that have been answered. The reason they usually look like various body parts is because ex votos are often pleas for better health.

Ex votos are most often seen in Catholic chapels, and can be a strange sight if you're unfamiliar with the practice. The term "ex voto" is short for the latin phrase e*x voto suscepto*, meaning "from the vow made."

Left: Fasces (top), Winged hourglass (bottom), Eye of God (mid), Torches: Upright & Inverted (far right.)

EYE OF GOD: A single eye with shafts of light radiating from it, or a single eye in the middle of a triangle, is called the "Eye of God," or the "Eye of Providence."

This is a symbol of God's omniscience, his power to know all and see all. The triangle stands for the Holy Trinity, and sun's rays are symbolic of God's glory. The Eye of God is often associated with the Masons (See Chapter 16.)

F

FASCES: Fasces is the Latin word for bundle, and usually refers to a bundle of wood rods wrapped by a cord. It symbolizes power through united effort, as well as governing powers.

FIRE: (See: Flame.)

FIREMAN'S HAT: A vocational emblem for a fireman.

FISH: Like the anchor, the fish was a secret symbol for early Christians. Another reason that fish represent Christ is that the first letters of the Greek word for fish, *ichthys,* can be used as an acronym for: Iesous Christos Theorou Yios Soter, which means "Jesus Christs, Son of God, Savior."

FISH WITH AN EYE INSIDE IT: This symbol refers to St. Raphael's journey with Tobias during which the saint taught the young boy the healing arts (See Chapter 13.)

FISH WITH BREAD LOAVES: Fish are often depicted with bread loaves around them or perhaps feeding on bread. Referring to when Jesus fed the masses with bread and fish.

FLAG: Often denotes military service. If it's not an American flag, the nationality of the flag may denote the country where the deceased was originally born.

FLAG, DRAPED OR FOLDED: This is a mortality symbol. A draped flag may represent someone who lost their life during battle.

FLAME: As a cemetery symbol, flames most often represent eternal life, eternal vigilance and/or religious fervor (literally a burning desire to know God.) However, when flames are seen around the borders of Puritan's headstones, they are a stern reminder to avoid the flames of Hell.

FLAME, UPSIDE DOWN: Items turned upside down is a direct reference to death. The flame that continues to burn when upside down refers to the eternal flame of the soul.

FLEUR DE LIS: In America, the fleur-de-lis is associated with the state of Louisiana and the city of New Orleans. As a ancient royal design, it is meant to represent a stylized lily flower. It has three petals to represent the Holy Trinity.

FOO DOGS: Lions are not native to China, so when the first Buddhist missionaries tried to describe the king of the jungle to the craftsmen of China, the end result is what we now call "Foo dogs."

Foo dogs are often seen at the gates of Chinese cemeteries, as well as many Chinese restaurants. The male foo dog sits on the right as you enter the gate. Under his left paw, he is holding down a ball, which is often painted gold. This ball represents the earth, and man's dominion over his family's worldly affairs.

Meanwhile, the female foo dog sits on the left side as you face the gate. Beneath her paw, she holds down a kitten to symbolize how women rule domestic life, and child rearing.

Griffin (left), Foo Dogs: Female (mid) & Male (right)

G

GLOBE: The earth. (See Ball.)

GRIFFIN/GRYPHON: A griffin (also spelled gryphon) is a mythical beast with the head, wings and claws of an eagle, but the head and body of a lion.

To Christians, a griffin symbolizes the duality of Jesus Christ as both a mortal and divine being. A male griffon does not have wings, but horns and a spiked tail.

H

HAMMER: If the hammer is seen on its own, it may be a vocational symbol, indicating a blacksmith or other laborer. It may also stand for the power of creation. A hammer on a book refers to the power of God's word.

HANDS: (See Chapter 12.)

HARP: When a harp is engraved on a headstone, it's usually a reference to heavenly music and praising the Lord. However, look closely; sometimes the harp is made to look as if one of the strings is broken, thereby indicating that a person's life was cut short.

Since Saint Cecilia (See Chapter 13) is the patron saint of music, further research into the life of the deceased may reveal they played an instrument, or if they were Catholic, they may have had St. Cecilia as their "name day."

The harp may also indicate a person with Irish ancestry, because it is one of Ireland's official symbols. As such, the harp is featured on the Irish passport and Euro coins. However, if you're a beer drinker, you've probably noticed the stylized harp in the Guinness logo.

HELMET: Helmets usually imply military service, but as a symbol they may also signify protection.

HORSE: A horse often indicates military service. Symbolically, horses represent generosity and courage.

HORSESHOE: The horseshoe is a well-known symbol for good luck even in this day and age. Americans of English and Irish descent often prefer to hang the horseshoe so that it makes a U shape to keep your luck from running out. Other European immigrants, however, hang it the other way so that all the good luck will pour down on you.

HOURGLASS: An hourglass is a blunt reminder that our time on earth is limited. On older stones, you may also find a Latin phrase such as *tempis fugit* (time flies) to further emphasize the point.

HUMMINGBIRD: While Aztecs believed great warriors reincarnate as hummingbirds, when seen on modern headstones, hummingbirds simply mean the deceased enjoyed these beautiful little birds.

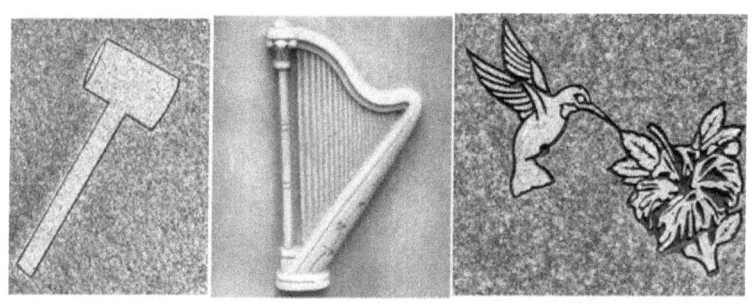

Left to right: Hammer, Harp, Hummingbird

K

KEY: Keys may symbolize freedom, or secret knowledge which can be the key to understanding something larger.

When a pair of keys are crossed, it refers to St. Peter, since he was given the keys to the kingdom of Heaven in the book of Matthew. If you see a male figure holding a set of keys (winged or not), it's probably St. Peter.

KEYSTONE: In architecture, you can't create an arch without a keystone in the middle to lock all the other stones in place. As a symbol, a keystone represents an important idea or belief from which you create a meaningful life.

The keystone is often a Masonic symbol (See Chapter 16.)

L

LABYRINTH: This is most often a Buddhist symbol showing the arduous path the human soul must take to achieve the blissful state of Nirvana.

LADDER: When a ladder is shown ascending into Heaven (clouds) it is called Jacob's Ladder, after the biblical tale of Jacob's heavenly visions.

A ladder may also be a reference to the crucifixion, since a ladder was used to take Christ's body off the cross. Ladders may also be used as a Masonic symbol. The clue here is that the letters C,H, and F (standing for Charity, Hope and Faith) will appear between the rungs.

LIZARDS: Ancient Roman graves used the lizard to symbolize hope for the afterlife. By the Middle Ages, Christians had adopted the lizard to symbolize resurrection and purification of the soul through religious faith.

LAMB: Since ancient times, baby sheep have been used in sacrificial ceremonies. So as a symbol, lambs represent innocence and sacrifice. Once again, this taps into lambs as a symbol of sacrifice. Here's a bit more about lambs:

LAMB ON CHILD'S GRAVE: On a child's grave, a seated lamb (so young that it has not yet had its tail bobbed) stands for an innocent soul. These are most commonly found on the graves of young children, although (I did see a lamb on the headstone of a 21-year-old man. A historian I spoke to suggested that this fellow may have had an intellectual disability that made him appear child-like and innocent.)

LAMB STANDING UP: When a lamb is standing up, or sitting next to a robed figure, you may be looking at a statue of St. John the Baptist, since in the Bible (John 1:29) he calls Jesus, "the Lamb of God who takes away the sin of the world."

LAMB WITH CROSS, BANNER OR HALO: A lamb with a cross, banner, and/or halo is known as the Lamb of God or Agnus Dei. This symbolizes the suffering of Christ on the crucifix as he sacrificed himself for the sins of mankind.

LAMP: Just as the flame of a lamp dispels darkness, the 'flame' of wisdom dispels ignorance. A lamp may also symbolize faithfulness, religious zeal, and the immortality of the soul.

LION: If you've ever seen "The Wizard of Oz," then it probably comes as no surprise that the king of the jungle often represents courage when seen in a graveyard. A single lion collapsed on a grave may represent a fallen hero.

Lions may also signify God's power and the strength to combat evil. A pair of lions often suggests wealth and pride in a strong family lineage.

Left to right: Seated lamb, Standing lamb, Lamp

M

MENORAH: (See Candles.)

MIZPAH: *Mizpah* is Hebrew for "watchtower." In the Victorian Era, jewelry bearing the word "Mizpah" was quite popular. Friends or lovers might wear a matched set created from a single coin emblazoned with the word, along with the Bible passage from Genesis 31:49: "And Mizpah; for he said, The Lord watch between me and thee, when we are absent one from another."

In graveyards, the word "Mizpah" may appear on its own, or perhaps next to a watchtower. It refers to the emotional bond remaining between the living and the dead.

MOTHER AND CHILD: A robed female figure holding a child or two may symbolize the Charity, who is one of the Seven Virtues (See Chapter 13), however, it may also symbolize a mother and child who died together.

N

NAIL: Even though four nails were needed to crucify Jesus, when shown on their own as a symbol, you nearly always see a grouping of three nails. This is to symbolize the Holy Trinity.

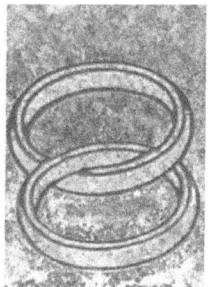

Left to right: Owl, Pitcher, Rings

O

ORB: (See Ball) In ancient Rome orbs symbolized royal power. When it appears with a cross attached to it, it represents Christ's dominion over the earth. On its own, it may simply represent earthly existence, or perhaps the cosmos, itself.

OSTENSORIUM: Also called a "monstrance," an ostensorium is the image of a sunburst with a circle in the middle. The circle symbolizes a communion wafer, and the sunburst stands for God's glory.

When you see an ostensorium on a grave, it means that the deceased was a member of the clergy.

Owl: The idea of a wise owl dates back to ancient Greece, where the owl was associated with Athena, the goddess of wisdom. In the graveyard, owls stand for wisdom, solitude, and watchfulness. As a Christian symbol, owls have the added symbolism of reminding the faithful that Christ can guide our souls even through the darkest of times.

P

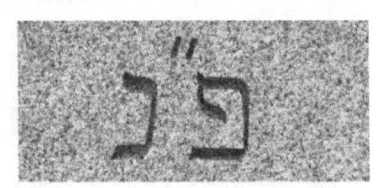

Hebrew letters: Pey & Nun

PEACOCK: Since the colorful design of a peacock feather looks a bit like an eye, peacocks are used to symbolize the omniscience of God.

When a pair of peacocks is shown drinking from a communion chalice or standing on either side of the Tree of Life, they represent the dual nature of mankind, who is both a physical and a spiritual creature.

PEGASUS: Pegasus is an ancient Greek horse that flew out of the head of Medusa after she was decapitated by Perseus. As a graveyard symbol, the pegasus stands for resurrection, renewal and rebirth. It is also considered a sign of poetic creativity and fleetness of the mind.

PELICAN: In addition to being the state bird of Louisiana, pelicans are a Christian symbol for charity. This stems from the mistaken notion that pelicans feed their young through self-inflicted wound in their belly. Of course, naturalists later realized that pelicans have a pouch.

Even so, pelicans have come to symbolize self-sacrifice.

parental love, and Christ's sacrifice on the cross.

PEY AND NUN: *Pey* and *nun* are a pair of Hebrew letters commonly seen on Jewish headstones. The letters are an abbreviation for *po nikbar*, meaning "here lies."

PHOENIX: According to ancient Greek myths, the phoenix would build a nest from myrrh, light it afire, then leap into the flames. Once the flames die out, a baby phoenix steps from the ashes, to live and grow for a good 100 to 500 years (depending on who tells the story) before burning itself to a crisp again. Christians adopted the phoenix as a symbol of Christ's resurrection as early as the first century A.D.

PITCHER: Pitchers mean different things depending on where you are. If you are visiting a Jewish cemetery, then a pitcher at a grave site implies that the person descended from the tribe of Levi. (Levites washed the hands of their priests with water.)

If you are in the Christian section of a historic graveyard, pitchers likely represent a woman of strong moral character, someone who was exceedingly generous, self-sacrificing, and charitable. It can also mean she was a prohibitionist, so pay attention to the dates on the headstone to see if she lived during America's Prohibition Era (1920 – 1933.)

R

RAINBOW: Rainbows often symbolize God's promise to Noah that he would never again destroy the world by flood.

A rainbow may also signify the connection between Heaven and earth.

RAINBOW FLAG OR BANNER: In 1978, Gilbert Baker designed a flag with rainbow-colored stripes. Baker was an American artist living in San Francisco, and he hoped for his flag to become a symbol of the gay community. Baker's intended symbolism for the colors of his flag are: pink for sex, red for life, orange for healing, yellow for sunlight, green for nature, blue for art, indigo for harmony, and violet for the human spirit.

Hot pink was hard to find, however, when it came time to mass produce the flags. That's the only reason it was dropped from the line up. Indigo was also dropped from the original flag, as well, just to keep things even. I've not yet seen a gay pride rainbow on a tombstone, but I am sure they exist.

RED LETTERING ON CHINESE GRAVES: If you see a monument featuring red Chinese characters on it, this means that the person is still living. After burial, the red color will be removed and replaced with white.

RINGS: A pair of wedding bands linked together on a tombstone indicates the grave of a married couple.

ROOSTER: When seen on older monument, the rooster represents vigilance, awakening and resurrection. The reason roosters often adorn weather vanes is to signify how they keep an eye out for evil both day and night.

If shown standing near a male figure, you're looking at St. Peter. The rooster, in this case, refers to the time Jesus told St. Peter that, "The cock shall not crow, till thou has denied me thrice."

ROPE: Rope, when tied in a knot stands for strong relationships. When severed, it indicates the cessation of life.

ROSARY: A rosary is a string of beads with a crucifix attached to it. After every 10 beads another, larger one is added. In this way, Catholics use this special necklace to help them count how many prayers they have taken. Rosaries are so-called because the beads were originally made from rolled up rose petals, which made them quite fragrant.

Left to right: Scroll, Sunset, Star of David

S

SCALES: Scales stand for balance and fairness, and are often associated with those in the legal profession. When a female figure holds scales, you are looking at Lady Justice, when male, the figure is most likely St. Michael (See Chapter 13.)

SCROLL: In Christian cemeteries, scrolls represent the actions of our lives being recorded in Heaven. On a Jewish grave, scrolls represent the Torah, Judaism's holiest scriptures.

SCYTHE/SICKLE: Often brandished by a skeletal figure we call the Grim Reaper or the bearded fellow known as Father Time, a scythe is a blunt symbol of life cut short by the final harvest.

SERPENT: (See: Snake)

SEXTON'S TOOLS: When various combinations of coffins, shovels, picks and spades appear on a headstone, they are referring to sexton's tools. Sextons are in charge of overseeing burials and maintaining cemeteries. When sexton's tools are shown on a monument, it could be either a vocational reference or meant as a mortality symbol.

SHIP: (See: Boat)

SHOES: A pair of baby shoes is sometimes seen on the graves of young children. Usually, one of the shoes will be knocked over, to symbolize the loss of the child.

SNAKE

SNAKES: Context is especially important to consider here. A group of snakes at the feet of a male figure, for instance, may represent St Patrick driving the snakes out of Ireland. While some have taken this literally, others believe that in this case "snakes" are a metaphor for pagans.

SNAKE: In Christian cemeteries, snakes are often a reference to Eve's temptation in the Garden of Eden, and thereby they symbolize sin.

SNAKE BITING ITS TAIL: The symbol of a snake devouring its own tail is called an ouroboros. This circular symbol dates back to ancient Egypt. On headstones, an ouroboros stands for immortality, eternity and the never-ending cycle of life and death. In alchemy, the ouroboros refers to a closed chemical process used to purify substances, so it may also refer to the evolution of the soul.

SNAKE TWINED AROUND A ROD: If it's one snake, this is the Rod of Asclepius. If two, you're most likely looking at a Caduceus. (See Caduceus.)

SPIDER WEB: Symbolizes both human frailty and interconnectedness. And just like real spider webs, this image is often found in the edges and corners.

SQUIRREL HOLDING NUT OR ACORN: On modern stones this probably just means that the person liked squirrels, but in historic cemeteries, a squirrel holding an acorn symbolizes spiritual striving and meditation.

STAG: (See: Deer) Each winter, a male deer sheds his antlers, only to regrow a new set in the spring. For this reason, a stag symbolizes regeneration. Because antlers look a bit like tree branches, the stag may also be associated with the Tree of Life.

STAG WITH A CROSS BETWEEN ITS ANTLERS: While the stag-and-cross symbol features prominently on the logo for Jägermeister liqueur, when seen in the cemetery this symbolizes purity, solitude and victory over Satan. (See: Deer)

STARS

STAR WITH FIVE POINTS: A single five-pointed star most often stands for the Star of Bethlehem which guided the wise men to the birthplace of Jesus, and to symbolize divine guidance.

Additionally, the five points of the star are said to represent the five wounds Christ received during his crucifixion.

STAR OF DAVID: The Star of David is a six-pointed star that symbolizes the bond between God and mankind. It is used to represent members of the Jewish faith on US Military headstones, and is often seen on headstones in Hebrew cemeteries.

A GROUP OF 12 STARS: When a monuments features a scattering of 12 stars, it most likely refers to the the 12 apostles of Jesus Christ.

STARS AND MOON: This signifies the ascent of the soul into the heavens.

CRESCENT WITH EIGHT-POINTED STAR: This indicates that the deceased was of the Muslim faith.

SUN

SUN: Since every plant and animal relies on the sun, it is an ancient symbol for life itself. It is hard, however, to tell whether the sun engraved on a monument is meant to be rising or setting, so most depictions have a dual meaning.

SUN RISING OR SETTING: As a setting sun, this represents the end of life. As a rising sun, it symbolizes the promise of a new day in the eternal afterlife.

SUNDIAL: Like an hourglass, this is a mortality symbol that represents the passage of time.

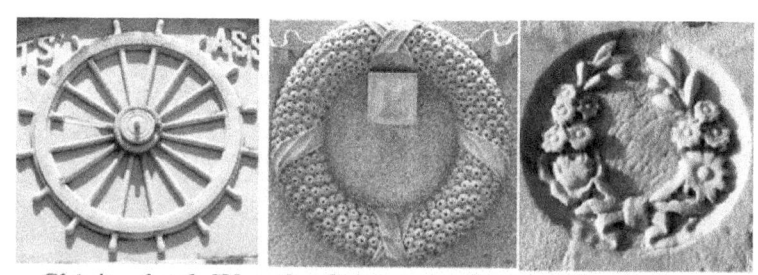

Ship's wheel, Wreath of poppy seed pods, Floral wreath

SWALLOW: Ancient Romans believed it was bad luck to kill a swallow because these were the birds that carried children's souls to the afterlife. This idea was later adopted by Christians who use the swallow to represent motherhood and the souls of departed children.

SWORDS:

SWORDS: When a female figure holds a sword in her right hand, this is Lady Justice, also known as Fortitude When a male figure wields a sword, it may be St. Paul or St. Michael (See Chapter 13.)
The sword is also part of the Immaculate Heart of Mary

   BROKEN SWORD: Much like a broken column, a sword shown with a broken blade represents a life cut short, and is most commonly seen on graves of veterans.

   CROSSED SWORDS: A pair of crossed swords often indicates a highly ranked military officer.

INVERTED SWORD: When the tip of a sword points down, it is said to be inverted. Symbolically, this represents relinquishment of power, as well as victory.

SWORD IN A SHEATH: When a sword is kept in its sheath it is a symbol of temperance and restraint.

T

TEAR VIAL: During the Civil War, women sometimes kept a lachrymatory (also called a tear vial, weeping bottle or tear catcher) to collect tears shed while their loved ones were at war.

These weeping bottles were also used for collecting tears when mourning the loss of children and other family members, not just soldiers. This practice gained popularity when Queen Victoria was seen using one after the death of her beloved Prince Albert in 1861.

TEMPLE: LDS members, a.k.a. "Mormons," who belong to the Church of Jesus Christ of Latter-day Saints sometimes engrave a picture of one of their temples on their headstones. The most commonly depicted Mormon temple is the one in Salt Lake City, but other ones maybe be shown, as well.

TEN COMMANDMENTS: Stone tablets, often engraved with Roman numerals one through ten, represent the Ten Commandments as received by Moses in the Bible.

TENT: In the Bible, the first places of worship were meeting tents, also called tabernacles. On a tombstone, a tent symbolizes a meeting with God. Several secret societies (including the Masons) use tents in their initiation rites.

TENT WITH THREE LINK CHAIN: When you see a tent with a three link chain, the tent represents the house of God, its open flaps symbolize inner truth, and the links of the chain represent the Holy Trinity.

TORCH: (See: Flame) The flame of a torch symbolizes the eternal soul. An inverted torch symbolizes the idea that a person's life is like a flame, and that even when this flame is extinguished by death, our soul continues to burn in the afterlife.

TRIANGLE: To Christians, the three sides of a triangle are yet another reference to the Holy Trinity. They may also stand for Faith, Hope, and Charity.

Left to right: Urn draped with a wreath & cloth, Urn with a flame, Wreath with Latin Cross & anchor

U

URNS:

URN: Urns were a very popular motif in America during the Victorian Era. Like so many of their symbols, the urn is borrowed from ancient Greece.

Ancient Greeks often cremated their dead and placed the ashes in ceremonial urns. At first glance, it seems rather ironic for the Americans to adopt the urn as a symbol in the 19th century, since cremation was rarely practiced until recently. Back then, people truly believed they would need their body to be intact on Judgment Day.

Even so, these Greek style urns are used to symbolically represent the idea of the mortal body being reduced to its barest elements as the soul ascends to Heaven.

While some sources I have read claim that the etymology of the phrase "gone to pot" can be traced back to the use of cremation urns, this does not appear to be a fact. "Gone to pot" actually refers to the practice of adding food scraps to a soup pot.

SHATTERED URN: This signifies old age.

URN WITH FLAME ON TOP: Stands for eternal remembrance and religious zeal.

DRAPED URN: If the cloth has a fringe, it represents the veil between life and death. If there is no fringe, then it represents the earthly garments being shed as the deceased moves from this world to the next.

URN WITH WREATH: Symbolizes mourning and eternal remembrance.

W

WHEEL: A wheel is symbolic of spiritual devotion and the never-ending power of God's creation.

BROKEN WHEEL: A broken wheel symbolizes that life's journey has ended.

WINGED WHEEL: A wheel with wings symbolizes the Holy Spirit.

Z

ZEBRA: Zebras are found on headstones for convicts and more frequently those who devoted their lives to mediating conflicts generated by two opposing groups of players who have differing views of the rule of the game.

Tui Snider

19 If You Enjoyed this Book

D id you enjoy this book? I certainly hope so! As an author, I depend upon word-of-mouth to spread the word about my creative projects.

If you like this book, please tell your friends and family, and consider giving a copy to them as a gift. Also, if you would take a moment to leave a review on Amazon and/or Goodreads, I would deeply appreciate it. Your opinion and thoughtful comments are extremely helpful in letting potential new readers know if this is the right book for them!

While you are there, check out the other books I have written. (You may especially enjoy my companion workbooks: *Graveyard Journal: A Workbook for Exploring Historic Cemeteries,* and/or *Ghost Hunters Journal: A Workbook for Paranormal Investigators.*)

If you are on social media, consider sharing a photo of your copy of this book, or even a photo of you and this book as you explore a historic graveyard. Tag your photos with #TuiSnider #GraveHour and @TuiSnider so that I can enjoy them and respond online.

Once again, I hope you had fun using this book and that it has been an enlightening adventure for you!

Sincerely,
Tui Snider
email: TuiSnider@gmail.com
website: TuiSnider.com

20 FURTHER READING

Books:

Nancy Adgent, (2010) *Deep East Texas Grave Markers*, Stephen F. Austin State University Press, Nacogdoches, TX

Douglas Keister, (2004) *Stories in Stone*, Gibbs Smith Publisher, Singapore

Chris Woodyard, (2016) *The Victorian Book of the Dead*, Kestrel Publications, Dayton, OH

Kenneth L. Untiedt, (2008) *Death Lore: Texas Rituals, Superstitions, and Legends of the Hereafter*, University of North Texas Press, Denton, TX

Mitchel Whitington, (2006) *Angels of Oakwood: Jefferson's Historic Cemetery*, 23 House Publishing, USA

Joseph Piercy, (2013) *Symbols: A Universal Language,* Michael O'Mara Books Limited, London, England

Andrew T. Cummings, (2003) *All About Symbols*, Astrolog Publishing House Ltd., Israel

Terry G. Jordan, (1982) *Texas Graveyards: A Cultural Legacy*, University of Texas Press

Marilyn Yalom, (2008) *The American Resting Place*, Houghton Mifflin, New York, NY

John Michael Greer, (2009) *Secrets of the Lost Symbol*, Llewellyn Publications, Woodbury, MN

Alexandra Kathryn Mosca, (2016) *Gardens of Stone*, CPI Group, UK

Christina Eriquez, (2009) *Our History In Stone*, Sinematix, Brookfield, CT

Sharon Baugher and Richard F. Veit, (2015) *The Archaeology of American Cemeteries and Gravemarkers*, University Press of Florida, Gainesville, FL

James Caskey, (2013) *The Haunted History of New Orleans*, SUBtext Publishing, Savannah, GA

David Fontana, (2010) *The New Secret Language of Symbols*, Duncan Baird Publishing, London, England

Mark O'Connell and Raje Airey, (2005) *The Complete Encyclopedia of Signs & Symbols*, Hermes House, London, England

Douglas Keister, (1997) *Going Out in Style*, Facts On File Publishing, New York, NY

David Bellingham, (2002) *An Introduction to Greek Mythology*, Quantum Publishing Ltd., London, England

Miranda Bruce-Mitford, (2004) *The Illustrated Book of Signs and Symbols,* Barnes & Noble Books, New York, NY

Clare Gibson, (1996) *Signs & Symbols*, Saraband Inc, China

Robert Florence, (1997) *New Orleans Cemeteries*, Batture Press, New Orleans, LA

Robert Florence, (1996) *Cities of the Dead*, University of Southwestern Louisiana, New Orleans, LA

Edgar Lee Masters, (1919) *Spoon River Anthology*, Prestwick House Literary Touchstone Classics, Clayton, DE

Ryland Brown, (2014) If The Stones Could Speak, Gateway Seminars, USA

Bill Harvey, (2003) *Texas Cemeteries*, University of Texas Press, Austin, TX

Jeremy Broussard, (2010) GraveHouse Legends, Corvus Press, USA

Gaylord Cooper, (2009) Stories Told in Stone, Motes Books, Louisville, KY

Kevin J. Bozant, (2015) Cryptic New Orleans, Po-Boy Press, New Orleans, LA

DA Goodrich, (2003) *Cemetery Art & Symbolism in North America*, Davis, CA

Websites:
https://www.elks.org/
http://www.masonic-lodge-of-education.com/
http://www.evangelicaltruth.com/es-htm
http://www.shrinersinternational.org/Shriners/History/Emblem
http://blog.southerngraves.net/2008/12/southern-cross-of-honor.html
http://hometownbyhandlebar.com/
http://spookylittlehalloween.com/
http://www.hauntjaunts.net/
https://www.va.gov/

www.ingramcontent.com/pod-product-compliance
Lightning Source LLC
LaVergne TN
LVHW010344050325
805083LV00001B/175